# Fifty Birds

# In

# Fifty States

## By James McVoy

Table of Contents

# Chapter 1
## The quest begins
## Introduction and ground rules

My serious birding life began innocently enough in 1986 with hiking at Ridley Creek State Park, an area of forest and meadows situated about thirty miles west of Philadelphia and a twenty minute drive from my apartment. The hiking started as a way to exercise and take a break from some personal problems. During my walks, I encountered a number of interesting birds that I was unable to identify, so I bought my first field guide: *Birds of North America, Eastern Edition*. It was published by Macmillan but is now out of print, which is a shame really. The book was very useful for a rank beginner like myself, not being organized taxonomically as most field guides are. Besides groups of ducks and hawks and gulls (which even I could separate from one another) there were sections titled "Red Birds", "Large Grayish Birds", "Small Grayish Birds", "Tree Clingers," – categories a new birder might actually be able to relate to! In those first exploratory rambles I wasn't aware of the larger birding community. I was just a guy with time on his hands and a healthy curiosity.

When Sue (my LAST wife, as she describes herself) and I started dating in 1995, she indicated an interest in my birding activities. Our first real birding excursion as a couple was a mini-pelagic[1] trip out of Cape May, NJ in March of that year. Planning to go on my own, I had been whining about having to get up at three a.m. and drive a hundred miles plus, making my way home completely exhausted late in the day, Sue suggested she could go along and share the driving. There were still spaces available on the boat so I booked one for her. It was a pleasant surprise that she

---

[1] Pelagic birds spend most of their lives out on the ocean. One needs to go out on a boat to see most of them.

was interested in going along. We had no idea that this was going to be the start of a lifelong hobby. Not to mention our relationship. We only saw eight species from the boat – Bufflehead, Long-tailed Duck, Razorbill, Surf Scoter, White-winged Scoter, Northern Gannett, Common Loon and Red-breasted Merganser. Sue somehow missed the Merganser, but she had seen seven life birds and they were all "good ones."

It was bitterly cold, which was to be expected in March off the coast of New Jersey. But we had a good time. On the way home Sue was driving up Rte. 55 across the middle of New Jersey, and I fell asleep. "SNRRKK." I snored myself awake and surprised the hell out of Sue, who nearly went off the road. We had a good laugh. Then I fell back asleep...and did it again!

One of the places I had birded quite a few times before we met was Tyler Arboretum, near Media, PA. It consisted of about 650 acres of open fields and forest fragments and planned plantings and included more than twenty miles of walking trails. I had seen several life birds there (I was still pretty much a beginner,) and Sue had never visited. So we decided to go there for a hike.

At one point during our walk, I suggested a brief rest on one of the benches out in the middle of a meadow: I had an ulterior motive. There was a personal story associated with that bench. Just two years earlier (before I met Sue) I had been birding that same area and had experienced a minor identity crisis. My thoughts that day ran something like, "What am I doing here? I 'm forty-seven years old and here I am traipsing around with a pair of binoculars looking for birds. This is nuts."

As I sat there on that earlier May morning having those dark and ugly thoughts my first Indigo Bunting landed on a bush almost literally under my nose. Well, it was in a bush right in front of the bench. You get the idea. That little electric-blue bird dazzled me and

6

basically answered the question about what I was doing out there – looking for the unexpected and the wonderful, tuning in to a world that I had lost some time back in my youth – that was what birding was all about for me. Oh, and those silly doubts have never come back.

"Hey, Baby, would you like to see a Green Heron?" Sue likes to tell new acquaintances that she married me for that unforgettable pick-up line. To tell the truth, that isn't exactly how it happened. That line came some months after we had been dating and birding together. May 3, 1995 to be exact. Why do I know that with such precision? For more than thirty years I have kept a fairly regular personal journal. When I finally joined the ranks of word processing geeks, I transcribed them all and now I can look up the most obscure events in my life in an instant.

Sue was working as a cabbie[2] at the time. I was working in my office at West Chester University that morning when the phone rang.

"Well, I'm toast for the day. The brakes just went in my cab, and the company doesn't have a backup vehicle for me to drive. I won't be making any money today."

"Hmm. Too bad. I was just checking the birding hotline and there is a report of a Swallow-tailed Kite being seen up near Bowmansville. Any interest in driving up look for it?"

"Might as well. I'll pick you up in a few minutes."
While waiting to be picked up, I printed out the report from PABIRDS. The Swallow-tailed Kite is normally found along the Gulf Coast and rarely strays into Pennsylvania. The email contained very specific directions to the location where the bird had most

---

[2] She had decided to finish her degree in her forties, and driving gave her the flexible schedule she needed.

recently been seen. We had begun to explore the wider birding community.

Sue picked me up and we set off for Bowmansville – Sue drove while I navigated. As we approached the reported location, there was a line of birders with scopes and binoculars scanning the skies. Must be the right place. We birded some brushy areas in the vicinity and flushed a Merlin, which was a nice bird indeed. Eventually the Kite showed up and we decided to head back home.

As we got into Sue's car, I asked "Have you ever seen a Green Heron?" I confess it had crossed my mind to try to impress my new sweetie, but I DID know where a pair had nested for the previous three or four seasons. It was the first time I ever even *sort of* promised someone I could produce a particular species. She couldn't see my fingers crossed behind my back! In any event, we stopped at Marsh Creek State Park and walked up the trail below the dam. There, in the wetland bordering the creek and perched on a log was a Green Heron. And that, young fellows, is how you get chicks.

February 2, 1996 was Sue's mother's eightieth birthday, and we decided to organize a surprise for her. Paula and Rick (Sue's sister and brother-in-law) and their kids, Sean and Heather, would fly to Tampa and we would rendezvous at the airport. Our job was to rent a car that would hold the entire gang. We got a humongous Lincoln to accommodate everyone, and it worked out just fine.

Early mornings when everyone else was asleep, of course, Sue and I managed to do some birding at various locations around the Tampa Bay area. One stop was at Honeymoon Island where we walked the Osprey Trail and found, um, a lot of Osprey nests. With Ospreys on them. We also checked out a couple of other local parks and ended up finding 46 species. *The*

*Quest* had not yet begun, or we might have looked for four more...

Confession time. I started birding seriously in the middle of 1986 and at the beginning of 1996 the Eastern Meadowlark had been my "bogie" or "nemesis" bird for nearly ten years. Lots of birders have them. It is a bird that everyone else has seen, but you cannot locate for yourself. I had embarrassed myself numerous times asking other birders where I might find some. They usually looked at me quizzically and said something like, "They're all over the place. Just check the fields anywhere." Um, yeah. Sure. Sorry to trouble you.

Sue suggested that winter that since we were both trained musicians, we should simply memorize the song. Don't ask me why this had not occurred to me before, but it had not. We bought a CD of North American bird songs and by spring my ear was ready for a Meadowlark to reveal itself by singing.

On April 7, 1996 we were driving my old red Toyota pickup truck up Route 1 just north of Lewes, Delaware, having been birding all weekend, starting down the New Jersey coast on Saturday, taking the ferry from Cape May across to Lewes, Delaware on Sunday morning.  On the way from the ferry terminal to the main road, we spotted a big bird perched on a power line along the left side of the road. A large, bulky sort of a bird. A Great Horned Owl! He was definitely an unexpected bonus from the Gods of Birding, and a life bird for both of us.

The weather was rainy and misty. Foggy and chilly. Nasty and cold, even. Despite this, I had the window cracked on my side of the truck just in case there were any birds to be heard. Wait! What was that? Sounded like a MEADOWLARK! Screeeeech. That was the sound of my tires as I slammed on the brakes. Meadowlarks do not screech. They sing a sort of whistly-warbly song that still gives me a thrill.  We had

9

passed the bird. It was sitting on a wire behind us singing its heart out. I made a u-turn and we inched closer and got a much better look. Fortunately, there was not much traffic, because it was Easter morning. Of course, about two miles up Route 1 that morning we found a flock of fifteen or twenty Meadowlarks. That's how it works with bogie birds. Once you find one, you realize they really *are* everywhere. Sigh.

As with many great historical movements, the exact origins of *The Quest* are forever lost in the mists of time. I did some serious research into the journals I mentioned above and was able to locate the following entry:

*Monday, July 29, 1996*
*On Saturday Sue and I drove to Harper's Ferry. We went for a couple of reasons - to see the town and to get a start on our West Virginia bird list. We got thirty birds in West Virginia, and I got my 50th and 51st Virginia birds on the way back (finally spotted a Robin in VA!) Sue has 44 Virginia birds, so we'll just have to go back. We are shooting for fifty birds in fifty states. We already have over a hundred in Pennsylvania, New Jersey, Delaware and Maryland. I think we have fifty in New York and thirty-something in Illinois. Probably close to fifty in Florida. Will have to check that out later...*

At some undetermined time before that entry I had been tinkering with my Birder's Diary® database, pulling up species lists for Pennsylvania, New Jersey, Delaware and Maryland where we birded most frequently. As we chatted about our birdy travels, Sue remarked that I had never seen much of the U.S. My parents had recently taken a trip to Alaska as octogenarians to fulfill their personal desire to visit all fifty states. We thought our visits should include birding.

10

Hmm. Fifty birds in fifty states had a nice ring to it and The Quest was born.

Obviously, we couldn't look for fifty DIFFERENT birds in fifty states – don't ask how many non-birders have asked us that one. That would total 2500 species. That is more than twice the number tallied in the North America (minus Mexico) and Hawai'i. We just wanted a list of fifty species that we had seen in *each* state. That meant that every time we crossed a state line the tally would re-set. Our old friends, the European Starling and Rock Pigeon (the bird formerly known as the Rock Dove) could count all over again. The first twenty to twenty-five birds in each state were generally very easy to find. Around thirty birds the challenge got a bit keener – especially in states where we had budgeted only a limited amount of time. The last five or six sometimes got to be both challenging and frustrating. Some states were reluctant to give up fifty at all. Some of those were surprising. West Virginia comes to mind. Some gave up fifty birds in an hour or two. As with all birding adventures, we never knew until we got there. Oh, and one last thing. We both had to identify at least fifty birds in every state, even though we considered ourselves team birders. We knew it wouldn't do to call our quest Fifty Birds in Fifty States and then at the end have one of us say something like, "Of course, you only got forty-nine in New Hampshire." Not that either of us is that mean-spirited, but to prevent future marital strife, that was our rule. Speaking of "marital" – yes, we got married about two years into the quest.

Some explanations of a number of our personal conventions may be in order here. When we travel, we usually keep a list of birds seen while driving and refer to it as our "on the road" list, or OTR for short. In more than a couple of states the OTR list has been crucial for getting our fifty birds. We also refer frequently to the Gods of Birding. Not that we believe in actual metaphysical gods who lead us to specific birds, but we use it more as an indication of our occasional and incredible good luck when we find something really special or witness one of those wonderful moments of bird behavior that we thought we would only read about in books.

Speaking of quirky, our mathematics can be very idiomatic at times. For example, one day we were playing the "Top Ten" game, as in "What are your top ten favorite birds in North America?" We each came up with thirty-five birds for our top ten lists. There would have been more, but we quit at thirty-five. We probably have closer to fifty birds in our top ten all-time favorites. We have no problem with the philosophical and mathematical contradictions inherent in these lists.

While I'm on the subject of math, I have to confess that my daily notes as we bird were sometimes slightly off the mark. I would announce proudly that we had already found fifty birds, say, in South Carolina, only to discover later that I had written down Barn Swallows twice and we really were one short. Or, there was the time in New Mexico when I forgot to write down a Bald Eagle. Seriously. When we traveled at first we would try to get a few extra birds in the close states in case my count was off. After a while I started printing out state checklists from my copy of Birder's Diary® and marking the little boxes with an "X" – that helped some. Sue finally bought a laptop computer for me in August of 2005 as a sixtieth birthday and Christmas present combined. (Actually, she said it was my birthday and Christmas present for the next ten years.) That helped keep the counts more accurately (assuming I typed in the correct information) and allowed me to type up my journal notes at the end of every day.

Once we got serious about the quest, Sue's love of planning trips really blossomed. She could often be found surrounded by a road atlas, an old copy of *Where the Birds Are*, various web page goodies (mostly information about National Wildlife Refuges for some reason) as well as airline schedules and hotel information. Since planning is NOT one of my strengths, I let her go ahead. During the early years of the quest, when we were still working (we both retired by the start of 2005), she had the extra restriction of planning around our spring breaks (sometimes fall breaks) and summer vacations. Since we both worked at West Chester University, at least our vacation schedules coincided.

In early July, 1996, we visited Chincoteague Island off the coast of Virginia. The big attraction for most tourists who stop there is the herd of wild ponies. We walked a couple of trails, one through a wetland and another through a forest fragment. While admiring a singing Eastern Meadowlark who was perched atop a large bush, we were approached by a fellow birder.

"Excuse me, I hear a Meadowlark, but can't seem to spot it. Can you point it out?"

"Sure, check the top of that large bush to the right of the tree over there."

"Got it! Thanks."

"You know, we keep hearing a Bobwhite on the other side of the trail, but haven't been able to locate the bird. Have you seen it?"

"Come over here."

With that, he pointed to a spot about twenty feet up in one of the trees lining that side of the trail. There was the Bobwhite, singing his heart out. Our mistake was looking for him on the ground. We had never thought to look that high up in the trees. At least not for a Bobwhite.

Later in the morning we were walking a path in a wooded area that was teeming with wild ponies and tourists. Our eyes wandered among the upper parts of the trees and were rewarded with a wonderful look at four Great-horned Owlets lined up on a branch. They were terribly white and fuzzy and cute. Sort of like gigantic cotton balls with huge eyes and tiny beaks. As we trained our binoculars on them, Sue said, "What is that reddish-brown bird just behind the owlets?"

I whispered, "It's an adult Eastern Screech-Owl! Wow. He looks just about the same size as the great-horned babies. What a treat!"

On our way home from Chincoteague, we stopped at Bombay Hook in Delaware. It is still one of our favorite birding spots anywhere we have been. Unfortunately in July the green-headed flies are numerous and deadly and nearly impossible to avoid. Despite being unable to open the windows of our car, we spotted a group of Black-necked Stilts, one Wild Turkey, two Ring-necked Pheasants, and a couple of Blue Grosbeaks.  It was almost worth fighting the green-heads. The operative word there is "almost."

## Chapter 2
## Virginia and North Carolina
## Tuesday, May 6 – Saturday, May 10, 1997

On May 3, 1997 Sue and I were married in the living room of my house on Darlington Street in West Chester. My folks were there as well as Sue's Mom. Also my two sons, Sue's niece and nephew, sister and brother-in-law. The next day Sue graduated from college, so we like to tell people that she got her Ph.D. before she got her bachelor's degree. You figure it out.

We delayed our honeymoon trip for several days while Sue took her mother to visit nursing homes in the Philadelphia area. Her mom had come up from Florida for our wedding, and it seemed logical for her to take care of this chore while she was in the area. That is what she told us, in any case. We might have planned it a bit differently, but at ages 50 and 51, the urgency level to get going was lower than it would have been when we were, say, twenty-five years younger.

The Outer Banks was our targeted area for the trip. It was reputedly beautiful, neither of us had been there, and most importantly there were a lot of birds to be found there. By now *The Quest* was firmly entrenched in our minds and this trip was planned (by Sue, of course) to finish up our Virginia birds and get our quota in North Carolina. We already had 38 birds on our Virginia list from the trip to Chincoteague the previous July.

Our first birding stop was at the Eastern Shore of Virginia National Wildlife Refuge. Strategically located at the tip of the Delmarva Peninsula, it sits at the narrow end of a natural funnel for migratory birds. Of course, that is mostly a fall phenomenon, but there were still plenty of birds to see. We only had a couple of hours to spend there, since we had reservations to spend the night in historic Williamsburg.

15

Speaking of strategically located, one reason there is a National Wildlife Refuge there now is because most of the land was acquired by the federal government near the start of World War II for military purposes. An installation was built there and eventually named Fort John Custis. If that name has a vaguely familiar ring, it might be because Martha Washington's first husband was a Custis. Same family, even. The military left in 1981 once the threat of an attack by German submarines was deemed unlikely, and the wildlife refuge was created in 1984.

On our way in to the parking area for the refuge a Bald Eagle flew right across in front of our car. This was taken as a good omen from the Gods of Birding. Out of the nearly 1,300 acres constituting the refuge we visited maybe one percent. We walked one of the nature trails bordering some grassy and marshy areas and managed to locate and identify forty-four species. Adding the new species to the list from our previous visit to Chincoteague Island, we now had 71 species for Virginia. Six states down, forty-four to go. This quest was going to take a while.

After leaving Eastern Shore National Wildlife Refuge we took the Chesapeake Bay Bridge-Tunnel to the mainland. Travelling on the bridge high above the water, we had the Atlantic Ocean to our left and Chesapeake Bay to our right. This trip was made in an earlier phase of American history, so we were able to stop along the way and look for birds. I'm pretty sure that after 9/11 such things were considered a security risk or at least suspicious. Our best birds on this leg of the journey were five or six Ruddy Turnstones. They weren't life birds, but they were new to our Virginia list. Plus they were very pretty.

We spent that night in Historic Williamsburg. Sue and I both have deep affinities for the 1700s. It was the age of George Washington and Benjamin Franklin. Bach, Haydn and Mozart. Sue is an avid fan of Franz

Josef Haydn, and I had spent eight summers of my professorial career teaching a course about the life and music of Mozart in Salzburg, Austria. Not just teaching, but reveling in the man and his miraculous imagination. There is something about the order and symmetry of the music of the Age of Reason that touches our souls in ways that defy explanation. Of course, we both have extensive training in music history and theory and also appreciate the quirky ways Haydn stretched the limits of harmony and form. We also marvel at the dazzling fecundity of Mozart's musical gift. But I digress.

Walking around town soaking up the eighteenth-century atmosphere, we enjoyed watching a fife and drum corps march and play their way down the street. We also enjoyed the fact that there was running water and indoor plumbing available at our hotel. Plus the stench of rotting garbage was missing from the streets. Oh, and cholera and smallpox were not a serious worry any more. I didn't say we wanted to actually LIVE in the seventeen hundreds, we just love the musical aesthetic of the time.

When dinner time rolled around we ate at one of the taverns. We were tired for some reason, so we returned to our hotel and went to bed early.

Wednesday morning we drove from Williamsburg down to North Carolina, and thereby re-entered the late twentieth century. A birding stop at Mackay Island on the way netted us over 40 bird species, so we figured our 50-bird list for the state would be a piece of cake. We camped at Manteo – Cypress Cove Campground, where they had a nature trail and observation deck.

On our first walk along the nature trail, we climbed to the top of the observation platform and watched an evidently young pair of Ospreys who, like us, were setting up their first home together. The campground owner had thoughtfully built a tower with a flat area on top for them to use. One reason we assumed they were new to the nest-building task was their tentative approach to the job. One of them would fly off and return with a sizable stick to add to the project. He or she would carefully place this in the rather random-looking pile and then the two of them would admire their progress. Sometimes the stick would simply slip off the tower and tumble to the ground. Sometimes it would add a small bit of bulk to the (to our eyes) pathetic nest. Mature Osprey nests can be massive and impressive. This one was more hope than substance.

At 2 A.M. I was struggling into my jeans in the confines of our tent, and for some reason, Sue woke up.

"What are you doing?" she whispered.

"Going to look for the Whip-poor-wills. Can't you hear them?"
I stood up and buckled my belt. Slipped on a t-shirt.

"It's the middle of the night."

"They sound like they're just outside our tent."

"It's pitch black outside, Love."

"There are lights scattered around the campground."

The lights didn't help. She was right. It WAS the middle of the night. It WAS pitch black. The Whippoorwills kept calling, but the pole lights blinded me and absolute darkness cloaked the trees where the calls were coming from. I gave up and crawled back into the tent, somewhat abashed. To her credit, Sue did not say, "I told you so."

Birding for a couple of hours at Pea Island National Wildlife Refuge the next morning yielded forty-four species. We opted for a stroll along the North Pond Wildlife Trail which was easy to get to from the Visitor Center. Wandering along a dike between two of the ponds that are part of 1,000 acres of impoundments, we spotted Black-necked Stilts, Black-bellied Plovers, a

18

Belted Kingfisher and a Tri-colored Heron. In the surrounding fields were Eastern Meadowlarks, an Eastern Kingbird, and an Orchard Oriole. The refuge boasted of nearly thirteen miles of protected beach and we made a quick walk down it for a few hundred yards. Thirteen miles was more than we wanted to walk. We did spot some Brown Pelicans and a couple of White Ibis along there, though.

Cape Hatteras has always invoked in me visions of hurricanes and shipwrecks. Pirates and sand dunes. Blackbeard with lighted matches flaming in his hair to instill terror in the crews of ships he attacked. Sailing up and down the coast of the Carolinas in his ship the *Queen Anne's Revenge* while flying his personal flag that featured a skeleton with a spear striking at a heart dripping blood.

Our visit was a bit more subdued than that. The weather was crystal clear. We hiked the nature trail and explored the varied habitats and enjoyed wonderful views of the lighthouse, which was billed as the tallest in the U.S. at 196 feet from its base to the top. The spiral stripes were black and white, belying its nickname of "The Big Barber Pole" since barber poles were traditionally red and white – a reference to the "good old days" when barbers were authorized to bleed customers when that was believed to be medically beneficial. You may recall how that worked out for George Washington. The birding was not spectacular, but satisfying. We spotted a Sooty Shearwater plying the waters offshore. Along the beach we did hit a bonanza of terns that we don't find very often – Least, Gull-billed, Royal and Sandwich. For our money, our favorite critter of the day was a River Otter near the base of the lighthouse itself. They always seem to be having a lot of fun.

I have been an aviation geek of sorts from the time I flew model airplanes as a kid – you know, the kind that had actual tiny engines and you flew from hand controls attached to the plane by strings. The airplane flew around in circles until you got dizzy, and then it crashed and you fell down. On a bad day you might even make yourself throw up. That's how it worked for me anyway. At the time of this trip I had recently read a couple of books about the Wright Brothers, so we had to stop at Kitty Hawk to see the Wright Brothers National Memorial.

Amid the sand dunes and sprawling shore developments stands a 60-foot granite monument atop Kill Devil Hill (whose top is another 90 feet above sea level.) From the base of this monolith, one can see smaller stones marking the first few flights the brothers made in their cleverly-named machine, *The Flyer*. The human race's first baby steps into the air took place right on that hill. It was moving to walk from the top to the more-and-more distant markers and imagine Orville and Wilbur's exhilaration on that windy December day nearly a century before. Their longest flight of the day covered just 852 feet, but it was a start!

The visitor's center at the memorial was designed to resemble an airport terminal building. It housed various exhibits, including a replica of the 1902 glider as well as the 1903 engine-powered machine. There were also old photographs of the brothers and plaques explaining the early history of heavier-than-air flight. I was in aviation geek heaven.

Here is some free advice for new birders: Never start looking for a new birding place without filling your gas tank first. We drove all over the back roads in the neighborhood trying to find the reputedly good birding area of Alligator River NWR. Dirt roads. A few scattered shacks of poor folks. Dead end lanes that ended at a swamp. All the while we were nervously watching the gas gauge as it crept steadily toward that magic red line that means you are about to hear the warning dinger go off. Did I mention that there were no towns, let alone gas stations where we were? We finally gave up for lack of gas. The suspense was getting too much for us. We started imagining getting stranded at some isolated spot like Stumpy Point and hearing banjos plunking out the theme from *Deliverance* in the background. We finally found a service station, but we had to go all the way back to Rte. 64.

Instead of returning to Alligator River, we stopped at the Elizabethan Gardens on Roanoke Island and got some very good birds. Imagine a bird's nest about the size of the end of your thumb. In it sat a tiny bird who weighed about as much as your breath. She was a Ruby-throated Hummingbird and her nest was in a tree just a little above eye level. Clearly a consolation from the Gods of Birding for our near disaster at Alligator River. Another tree was adorned with no fewer than *three* male Scarlet Tanagers. It looked like Christmas. Sort of. I mean, the tree was not a conifer and the weather was too warm to be December. Other than that it was exactly like Christmas. Seeing three of those guys in one tree was a treat. A thrill even. Better than most Christmas presents. So there!

We left Manteo about 7:30 the next morning. Drove through the Great Dismal Swamp, but didn't see much birdlife. Of course the weather was pretty dismal and we were ready to get back home.

On our way we spent about an hour visiting the National Arboretum in Washington, D.C. We managed to find thirty species of birds. That, of course, made us wonder how and/or whether to include them in the quest: *Fifty Birds in Fifty States Plus Thirty or so in the Capital District.* That seemed a bit too long and asymmetrical for our eighteenth-century tastes.

## Chapter 3
## New Mexico the first time
## Thursday, December 31, 1998 – Saturday, January 9, 1999

By the end of 1998 the quest had really become serious, and Sue suggested that we needed to visit the Southwest. She was especially in love with New Mexico, feeling that the high desert somehow spoke to her spiritually. Personally, I find "spiritual" matters to be wishful thinking and what I refer to as "woo-woo." On the other hand, I had never visited that part of the country and it would be a chance to see some new birds.

*Where the Birds Are* suggested we focus on Bosque del Apache NWR south of Socorro, and Las Vegas NWR, near, um, Las Vegas. Not Nevada. New Mexico. We didn't know there were two of them, either. This Las Vegas is northeast of Santa Fe, if you don't feel like looking at a map. Both National Wildlife Refuges boasted great opportunities for birding.

After arriving at the Albuquerque Sunport, we picked up our green Chrysler Cirrus rental car and drove to our hotel just off I-40. Checked in for our first stay at the Best Western Rio Grande. The place was heavily paneled with dark wood worked into various Southwestern motifs – even the interior of the elevator, which always smelled heavily of furniture polish.

Driving around the interstates in New Mexico, you couldn't miss the fact that highway interchanges did not have to be simple gray tangles of concrete and steel. In Albuquerque the big ramps were painted in southwestern browns and pinks and blues with accents that reflected the native culture of the surrounding area. Too bad other areas haven't picked up on the idea. Imagine the interchanges in Philadelphia painted to look like giant soft pretzels or Houston's suggesting coiled lariats. Just a thought.

Another local oddity that caught our attention was a sign along I-40:

## GUSTY WINDS MAY EXIST

Ever since we first saw that sign in 1999, Sue and I have debated whether it might be one of those unanswerable existential questions. Perhaps a Zen koan. Maybe just the confused expression of *fin de siecle ennui*. Or, more probably, simply a quirky local version of "Caution: Cross Winds on Bridge."

After we freshened up a bit we drove over to Petroglyph National Monument on the northwest side of town. Picked up brochures at the visitor center then hiked around Rinconada Canyon. The trail at Rinconada started almost literally in someone's back yard. That section of the National Monument land bordered a typical suburban housing development. Honest-to-God ticky-tacky. Once the houses were left behind, the landscape consisted of desert scrub and rocks. The rocks were covered in places with hundreds of petroglyphs. Animals. Zigzag patterns. Birds. Human hands. The usual array of Native American symbols. It was estimated that the park area housed as many as 25,000 petroglyphs. We photographed dozens of them and wandered two or three miles through the desert. Along the way we got two life birds – Canyon Towhee and a Canyon Wren. One of the joys of visiting a new geographic location for the first time was that many of the birds that were common for the local folks were life birds for the visitor.

Drove back to Old Town for a brief wander. Ate at "Little Anita's New Mexican Food." Checked out the Western Warehouse, where I bought a new cowboy hat on sale for $20. Had to. It practically jumped off the rack and begged me to take it home. Went back to our hotel to ID the birds (since we had forgotten our guide books that afternoon.) They were easy, fortunately.

23

Our neighbors in the hotel were extremely rowdy during the night. You'd think they could find a better place to celebrate New Year's Eve than a motel room! We finally complained and they quieted down at about a quarter to three. We got up around five and were on the road by 5:35. Tired and grumpy. Headed south on I-25. Stopped for a big breakfast a few minutes after six.

The high desert south of Albuquerque stretches out on both sides of I-25, interrupted by occasional mountain ridges. The reds and browns and grays were not colors I was accustomed to seeing as part of a general landscape. Where I came from shades of green dominated. The road was so straight I imagined setting the cruise control and taking a nap. Mile after mile rolled by with only occasional exits for towns with names like Los Lunas and Belen and Socorro. Emily Dickinson's poem, *The World – feels Dusty* crept into my mind.

> *The World — feels Dusty*
> *When We stop to Die —*
> *We want the Dew — then —*
> *Honors — taste dry —*

We started finding interesting birds along the road south of San Antonio – a few Sandhill Cranes, some Gambel's Quail (wonderful.) Both lifers, of course. Got to Bosque del Apache a little before 8. Our first new bird at the refuge was a Say's Phoebe. Followed by a Sedge Wren. There were a lot of Kestrels, Red-tailed Hawks and Harriers at the refuge as well as thousands of Sandhill Cranes and Snow Geese. We already had over thirty-five birds on our New Mexico list. We figured we should get our fifty handily before we were done. Checked in to the Casa Blanca B&B that afternoon – planned to rest up and go back to the refuge later.

At one time San Antonio was a prosperous town, a home to ranchers and miners and the birthplace of

24

the hotelier Conrad Hilton. Now it seemed more like the proverbial wide spot in the road. Casa Blanca was one of the largest Victorian-style farmhouses in the area. It was built of double adobe with a typical tin roof and a large veranda. The house passed through many families over the years until it was purchased by Phoebe Wood in 1988. The home was opened as a bed and breakfast in 1989 and had been operating continuously ever since.

It was a couple of blocks off the main beaten path. Phoebe, our hostess was a petite blonde in her mid-fifties who described herself as retired from working for the public schools (she did not say she was a teacher.) She seemed bookish and quiet, and a child of the sixties for sure. She grew up in the Philadelphia area and attended Syracuse University, MY alma mater! After SU she joined VISTA and spent 14 years working on Indian reservations in the Southwest.

Phoebe had three pets at the time. Ebony, an all-black cat with some Siamese blood had the slim Siamese build and a propensity to talk a lot. He also had one very long canine tooth while the other is missing. This gave his face a somewhat comical look reminiscent of Bucky in *Get Fuzzy*. He had a beautiful coat, though. There was also an orange cat named "Phillipe" with long hair and a part-Persian look about him. He was not as sociable as Ebony, so we didn't see much of him. Dakota was a stray dog who had joined the household a couple of months earlier. She was a quiet Lab-Rottweiler mix (probably.) Very friendly and very sweet and definitely very, very old.

The B&B itself had three guest rooms and two "common rooms." The old walls were about two feet thick, which insured sound isolation as well as insulation from the outside cold. Our room was decorated in a typical Southwest style, sporting a wood stove, a modest wardrobe and a double bed. We had a private bathroom and a south-facing door that opened on to the parking area beside the house. It was all very cozy and conveniently close to Bosque del Apache. Outside our room was a large platform-style bird feeder that was a faithful reproduction of Casa Blanca itself.

Like many National Wildlife Refuges, Bosque del Apache had a loop road that allowed limited access to parts of the refuge. The ninety-square-mile refuge was bisected by the Rio Grande. Besides the river itself, there were numerous impoundments that were carefully managed to provide appropriate levels of water for different species at different times of the year. It was flanked by mountains that turned luscious shades of pink and purple at sunrise and sunset. Our first night the full moon came up huge and brilliant over the mountains and viewed through the silhouettes of the cottonwood trees it was dazzling.

We returned to the refuge around 3:30 and decided to drive all the way around in order to try to identify the cormorants we had seen earlier. Good thing. They turned out to be Olivaceous (or Neo-tropic) instead of Double-crested, and thus were life birds for both of us. We then proceeded around to the area we had been told a Whooping Crane has been hanging out. We found it! I still get goose bumps thinking about it. While we were in that area, I decided to scan a large flock of blackbirds. Most were Red-winged Blackbirds, but some were Brewer's and one turned out to be a Yellow-headed. So far we had seen 45 species including 11 lifers since the previous day. A great start for 1999! Wait! It was actually 46 species. I forgot to write down the Bald Eagles on the day list. Seriously.

The Whoopers were the last two of four who had been introduced to Bosque in the hope of starting a new migratory flock there. The two we saw met their demise very different ways. One was eaten by coyotes. The other flew into a power line and broke its neck. The project was abandoned.

We had an early coffee at Casa Blanca and took snacks with us. Got to Bosque before sunrise and hiked the Canyon Trail as the sun came up. It was very cold – heavy frost on the car. Warmed up by the time we finished the four-mile trail [according to my old-and-not-very-reliable pedometer] The scenery was breathtaking. The birds were absent.

We stopped back at the visitor's center when they opened at 8. Watched the informational movie about wetland management at the refuge. Bought Peterson's *Guide to Raptors*, refuge patches, and a few postcards. Then we returned to the access road and some serious birding.

We got six or seven life birds that day including our first Roadrunner, Sage Sparrows, Pyrrhuloxia, a Black Phoebe for Sue and a Ladderbacked Woodpecker. We were up to 66 or 67 New Mexico birds depending on whether the Spotted Towhee counted as a separate species from our Eastern Towhee. [It did.]

I nearly forgot to mention the coyote family we spotted that day. There were three adults near one of the large flocks of Sandhill Cranes. One was walking across the open field and stopped to touch base with the others. One of the others pulled rank and the first one we saw lay down and allowed the presumed Alpha to sniff him over while he lay on his back in total submission.

We had a dreadful dinner at a chain restaurant in Socorro and it was a toss-up whether the service or the food was worse. We decided not to get up at the crack of dawn the following morning. We were considering checking out Fort Craig and/or Water Canyon and/or the VLA Radio Telescope. It was only 7:30 p.m., but we had hiked about seven miles that day, so we were about ready to turn in.

We got up "late" – about 7:30 and had breakfast at Casa Blanca. Then drove up to Socorro and picked up a few goodies we needed. From there we headed out Route 60 west toward Magdalena. Decided to stop at Water Canyon in Cibola National Forest because Phoebe had suggested it was a good birding spot. It turned out to be a wonderful birding spot – we got Western Bluebirds, Mountain Bluebirds, Acorn Woodpeckers, Red-naped Sapsucker – lots of good stuff.

We continued on past Magdalena to the Very Large Array radio telescope. Twenty-seven eighty-two-foot-high radio dishes in the middle of the desert. Pretty impressive. Did I mention that I used to be a serious astronomy geek? I thought not. Along the way we saw a herd of about 30 pronghorn antelopes and stopped to take pictures.

On our return drive we stopped at Evett's Café in Magdalena for a bite to eat. This place was a slice of genuine Americana. A hand-lettered sign on one wall read "Gotta stop at Evett's... Veterinary Supplies; Cosmetics; Drugs; Sundries; Fountain; Real Western Hospitality." Another was an old advertisement with a young lady in a bathing suit looking as if she came right out of the 1940s – "Drink Nesbitt's California Orange." Two walls were lined with cases of antique junk – stuff like razor strops, a lard bucket, old adding machines and cash registers, a 1930 New Mexico license plate, and an old A&W root beer mug. There was a sign reading "THELMA - THE QUEEN OF PERFUMES" that I should have taken a picture of for my Mom, even though she hates her own name. Didn't, though. *C'est la vie*. We stopped at Water Canyon again and got a Mountain Chickadee and, um, oh yeah, a Golden Eagle.

Made a quick run down to Bosque in hopes they'd have *Roadside Geology of New Mexico*. They didn't, so I got a postcard with a roadrunner on it instead. Went back to Casa Blanca for a nap. Then back to Socorro for dinner at Val Verde – good food at a reasonable price. I had shrimp and chicken Dijon, Sue had prime rib.

When we returned to Casa Blanca I had to play *As Time Goes By* on Phoebe's out-of-tune piano. She dragged out her 1966 yearbook from Syracuse University and we looked for people we knew. Since we were around the same age, we started naming classmates and talking about what we did and what we majored in. Turned out that we sang in the same Chapel Choir for a year or two! She hauled out her old yearbook and turned to the group pictures. She was clearly visible in the soprano section. My back row seat was cropped out of the photo. I assured her that I was in there, though. Had a good visit until we all decided it was time for bed around 8:45. We only walked about 3 miles today.

Sue drove to Santa Fe the next morning – we took the Turquoise Trail up from Albuquerque. Lots of beautiful vistas and tacky little towns. We had planned to visit a group of museums that turned out to be closed on Mondays. So we went back into town, grabbed a bite to eat at the *Ore House on the Plaza.* Actually, it was a pretty big bite. I ordered the "Black and Blue Burger" – a blackened burger with blue cheese on a Kaiser roll with a side order of jalapeño potato salad. We were going to go to the *Atomic Café* for Atomic Burgers or some such, but it wasn't open. Then we wandered around the plaza shopping for wedding rings. Finally found mine at Turquoise Trail. It was a Navajo-crafted gold ring with turquoise and lapis lazuli. Sue found a tentative choice for herself, but we planned to look in Las Vegas. O yeah, I bought a couple of things at a bookstore downtown. *Southwest Essays* by Aldo Leopold and a Spanish *Winnie-the-Pooh.* I have a collection of *Winnie-the-Pooh* books in numerous other languages. I also got a CD of Latin American symphonic music.

**JAKE BRAKE USE PROHIBITED**
City Ordinance 1994-49

sign seen all over Santa Fe
(what is Jake Brake Use?)

Tuesday we drove out to Bandelier National Monument. The scenery was awe-inspiring. Wonderful sandstone formations and mountains and mesas. The park itself was very beautiful and we were virtually alone on the trail around the ruins. Along the way we saw Canyon Towhees, a Canyon Wren and three species of nuthatches in the same tree – White-breasted, Red-breasted and Pygmy (a lifer.)

Back in Santa Fe we went to the Plaza looking for a ring for Sue. Ended up buying one made by Tom Pine, the same Navajo craftsman who made mine. This evening we had dinner at Paul's. We had champagne to celebrate Sue's 300th North American bird and finally finding our rings. The food was terrific.

Our next stop was Las Vegas, NM. Got there around 11 AM. Our room wasn't ready, so we drove over to the National Wildlife Refuge. Most of it was inaccessible, but there were views of flat land and a number of small lakes. Saw a lot of raptors, including a Ferruginous Hawk (lifer.) Then drove back over to Las Vegas and checked out the town. Depressed and awful were the first adjectives that leapt to mind. We stopped at a bookstore owned by friends of friends. Had a longer visit than desired since most of the conversation dealt with the husband's failing health. We decided one night in Las Vegas would be more than enough so we cancelled our motel reservation for the next night. The plan was to try and book the next night in our hotel in Albuquerque. We would go birding at dawn and hit the road out of there. We had dinner at a local restaurant in Las Vegas and they won the prize for the worst meal of the trip. Not only was the food terrible, but a poor old

30

man who probably had had a stroke sat in the corner and moaned throughout dinner. Creepy.

Got up early and went to the wildlife refuge at sunrise. Nothing new, but a good look again at the Ferruginous Hawk. Also an adult coyote – I tried to take his picture – we'd see if it came out [It didn't.] Headed back to Albuquerque. Stopped at Santo Domingo Pueblo, but it was closed. Spent some time at the Bien Mur trading post – wonderful Indian art at reasonable prices (and they have a Web page.) Were going to take the tramway up the mountain, but Sue thought better of it. She doesn't like heights. Went to the Rio Grande Nature Center in Albuquerque and it was pleasant and had good birds – we got a couple of new New Mexico birds and one lifer for Sue – Bewick's Wren. That evening we checked out a bookstore at Nob Hill where I bought a biography of Billy the Kid. Dinner was at a fine Italian restaurant – Scala – great food and a violent contrast to the previous evening's debacle.

For our last day in New Mexico, we went back out to Petroglyph National Monument and hiked around Boca Negra Canyon. Saw a ton of wonderful petroglyphs and a few different birds (Northern Harrier, Red-tailed Hawk, Canyon Towhee, Sage Sparrow, and Western Meadowlark.)
Back in Albuquerque we wandered around Old Town. Bought a few gifts for folks back home. Stopped in at the bookstore in Nob Hill and picked up a dictionary of French slang and a copy of *Navajo Made Easier*. Easier than what is not clear. Dinner again at Scala – I ordered a salad and a half-order of calamari that was delicious. Back at the hotel we packed for our return trip and I read part of *The Saga of Billy the Kid*. My son, Ben, called to say there had been a lot of snow back home. He also said that he had not received the car keys we had mailed him several days earlier. Uh-

oh. Our car was at his place and he was supposed to pick us up at the Philly Airport.

The flights home were perfectly normal. When we got to the Philadelphia airport, Todd (my older son) picked us up. Seems the keys never had arrived and Ben's car was probably too small for us and our luggage. We took Todd and his wife, Julie, out to dinner at *Ruby Tuesday's* on the way home. Turned out the keys showed up in that day's mail, but it was too late to do Ben any good. Everything worked out OK anyway. I started entering our bird sightings into our database, but after a short stint decided I was too tired to be accurate. Maybe another day.

# Chapter 4
## South Carolina and Georgia
### Saturday, March 6 – Friday, March 12, 1999

Leaving home in the dark gets to be a habit with serious birders. Saturday morning there was a little light appearing in the east as we hit the road at 6:25. We made our way to I-95 and drove all the way to Santee, South Carolina, just off exit 102. The weather was overcast and gloomy pretty much until we got to the South Carolina border. Even though we shared the driving, we both got pretty groggy on the road. At one point in Virginia we pulled into a rest area. I thought the men's room was strange, since there were no urinals. Then I realized I had stumbled into the ladies' room. Oops.

Driving south across Virginia and North Carolina we were bombarded with a series of billboards advertising "South of the Border." In this case the border was the North Carolina/South Carolina state line. Exploiting the ambiguity of its name, the place had a decidedly Mexican flavor to it. Except, of course, everyone spoke English. Well, English with a Southern drawl. After driving most of the day we needed a break just about the time we crossed the border. The place included a huge "Sombrero Tower", souvenir shops, hotel rooms, a gas station, restaurants. We needed to fill our gas tank and as long as we were there, we checked out the kitsch in the souvenir shop before getting back on the road with a fresher driver. No, we didn't buy any Mexican souvenirs there.

We did make a brief stop at the Santee National Wildlife Refuge to get our bearings. Got a dozen birds for our South Carolina list, including Osprey and White Ibis before heading to our motel and a much-needed night's sleep.

We grabbed a quick continental breakfast at the hotel and headed back to the wildlife refuge just as the

33

eastern sky started showing the first hints of dawn. Santee NWR is comprised of more than 10,000 acres of wetlands and bodies of water interspersed with nearly 5,000 acres of mixed hardwood forests, pine plantations and agricultural land. In the midst of it all is the Santee Indian Mound which was also the site of a British fort during the American Revolution.

While hiking the trail near the visitor's center it was easy to imagine the comings and goings of the ancient Santee Indians who inhabited the area more than 3,000 years ago. Or to picture the Swamp Fox, Francis Marion, and Light Horse Harry Lee stealing through the swamps with their troops to surround and take the British position.

After our initial walk around we decided to make our way to the Cuddo Unit which offered a seven-and-a-half mile wildlife drive and the promise of opportunities to see birds as well as other local critters in various habitats. As I drove along beside one of the numerous channels, we spotted two enormous alligators. Well, I thought they were enormous, but this was my first actual encounter with ANY alligator, so they could have been average for all I know. They were at least ten to twelve feet long, and they were lying still in a narrow channel right next to the road. I grabbed my camera and quietly opened the car door. Slipped out and aimed at the leviathans.

"Crap!" I shouted something rather more colorful than that particular expletive. In fact, I let loose a stream of blue comments. The batteries in my camera had chosen this inopportune moment to let me know that they had, in fact, died.

Sue grabbed her camera and jumped out of the other side of the car in hopes that she could salvage the moment. Unfortunately, my outburst had spooked the 'gators, and they had let themselves disappear beneath the murky water. As it happened, Sue's camera had also lapsed into a coma, so we couldn't

have gotten a picture anyway. You guys shoulda seen the size of those things! Seriously!

The next morning we drove to Charleston and spent the afternoon walking around town. There was a large flock of Cedar Waxwings right in the middle of town. As we were walking down one street past a group of teen-aged boys, one of them thought it would be funny to suddenly jump up and scream in Sue's ear. We both pointed out the error of his ways, using a liberal sprinkling of the "F" word. As we were completing our loop of the old city (with beautiful buildings and parks and the faint odor of a paper mill) we found a camera shop and bought batteries for both cameras. Of course we were too tired to bother to retrace our walk, so we took nearly one picture of beautiful downtown Charleston. The weather was gorgeous all day – warm and sunny.

After Charleston we drove down to Hilton Head Island. We realized we had found our fifty birds for South Carolina and there was no motel nearby, so we headed back to I-95. We stayed near Hardeeville that night with plans to begin our search for birds in Georgia the next morning.

Our assault on the birds of Georgia began with an early morning drive to the Okefenokee National Wildlife Refuge. Sort of. The directions in Where the Birds Are led us to a Pogo Museum instead of the NWR. Not that I am not a fan of Walt Kelly's classic comic strip, but we wasted half the morning getting to the refuge. It was windy, so we saw very little other than a Pileated Woodpecker on the way in. We did see eight alligators – seven small and one medium-sized, but our Georgia bird list was still a long way short of fifty.

So we decided to drive over to the coast and try our luck there – saw two whole birds at Harriet's Bluff. Heading back to Savannah, we wound up at a motel on

Tybee Island. So far we had about 37 birds in Georgia. We planned to check out the wildlife refuge rumored to be in the neighborhood. Hope was fading for 50 Georgia birds on this trip.

We got going shortly after 6:30 the next day. Eventually found Skidaway Island State Park. It was on another barrier island with both salt and fresh water and the place promised many more birds than we were able to locate that day. We wandered around one of the hiking trails for a couple of hours and managed (just barely) to get exactly 50 Georgia birds.

After finally finding our fiftieth bird in Georgia, we started driving back towards South Carolina. Our goal was to get to Carolina Sandhills National Wildlife Refuge before dark so we could look for a Red-cockaded Woodpecker. It was a miserable drive. Heavy downpours off and on all day. The rain let up some later in the day, but it was still drizzly and misty when we got to the refuge. We drove and walked around until it was too dark to see birds. I did actually hear a Red-cockaded Woodpecker and Sue caught a glimpse of one as it flew into its nest hole. One of the nice features of the refuge was that the rangers had painted white rings around each tree known to have an active Red-cockaded nest in it. Of course, after dark that wasn't doing us much good, so we drove back to Hartsville and checked into a local motel.

At five A.M. the next morning we grabbed a quick breakfast so we could get to the refuge before dawn broke. We took up concealed positions near a marked nesting tree (with a silent "thank you" to whomever decided to mark them) and waited in the chilly pre-sunrise forest. We got colder and colder as the minutes crawled past. It was one of those gray dawns that don't break so much and ooze in. The light almost seemed embarrassed to push the dark aside.

Occasionally one of us would risk a peek around the trees we had hidden behind. At some point it crossed both of our minds that we were slightly nuts to be doing this. Around five minutes before seven, the Gods of Birding threw us the crumb we had come seeking. A male Red-Cockaded Woodpecker poked his head tentatively out of the nest hole. Withdrew. Peeked out again and exploded into the air, landing on a nearby tree. He had the decency to perch there for a good thirty seconds before flying off into the gloomy morning fog. Wow.

We hiked around the nearest trail in the cold and damp for another hour or so, but the birds were smarter and stayed concealed, and presumably warm.

After our successful visit to the Sandhills NWR we drove across North Carolina and into Virginia. Stopped at the Natural Bridge and hiked a couple of miles there. Continued to the vicinity of Luray Caverns where we spent the night. There was quite a lot of snow on the ground and a cold wind. We planned to see the caverns in the morning and then head for home.

We managed to see the caverns, and yes, they were spectacular. One of those experiences that make one realize how brief human life is when measured against geological time.

# Chapter 5
## Texas
### Friday, March 2 – Friday, March 9, 2001

One of the exciting aspects of going birding in a completely new place is looking through guide books and trying to guess what we might find. Of course, there is also the fun of picking out one or two "target" birds that one just HAS to see in that area. For us, one of the target birds for our visit to Texas was the Roseate Spoonbill. When we flew into Houston in early March, 2001 we landed around noon and immediately picked up our rental car and drove out to Brazoria NWR. Still don't know how it is pronounced. Bra-ZOR-ia. Bra-zo-RIa. Or some other accent. Doesn't matter.

In any case, Brazoria is one of three refuges – along with San Bernard and Big Boggy – in the Houston area that form a huge coastal haven for migrating species to and from Central and South America as well as a nesting ground for hundreds of others.

Arriving at the refuge around 2 PM Friday, we started to drive around the access loop. After nearly ten minutes of mind-numbing boredom and nearly a quarter of a mile into the seven-mile loop, we spotted a small flock of - YES! - Roseate Spoonbills. Might as well go home. But we only had a dozen or so birds for Texas at that point. By the time we finished driving the loop, we had 42 species. And that didn't include our On the Road list for the day. Besides the Spoonbills, the Gods of Birding granted a bonus for the day's efforts: wonderful looks at a White-tailed Kite. Magnificent. Superb. Fantastic. Cool, even. Other birds that we enjoyed particularly were the Sandhill Cranes, Loggerhead Shrikes, Greater White-fronted Geese and Blue-winged and Green-winged Teal. We get to see Green-winged Teal a lot back home, but Blue-winged are not all that common.

That evening we checked into a Ramada Inn in Lake Jackson. We were very tired, so we decided to eat in the house restaurant rather than look for someplace else. The food was surprisingly good, and we could walk back to our room within a few minutes of finishing dinner. Oh, and we ended the day with 48 Texas birds, so the quest part of the trip was already well in hand.

We got up early Saturday and drove to San Bernard NWR. The weather was heavily overcast with intermittent showers – not pretty. We saw some nice birds at San Bernard in spite of the rain. A Great-horned Owl was definitely the highlight. It was also bird number 49 for Texas.

We didn't get around to eating breakfast that morning until nearly ten o'clock. Gem's Pancake House in Bay City was still serving, so we stopped and enjoyed seeing some of the locals. Among the usual rednecks in pickup trucks and flannel shirts there was one bizarre fellow in a silly hat that beggared description. That means I forgot to write down anything about it and have since forgotten. Must have been incredibly memorable. In a silly way, of course.

Our next planned stop was at Aransas NWR. It is a huge refuge (more than 115,000 acres) and most of it is closed to the public. The parts that are open regularly produce good looks at a wide variety of wildlife – alligators, javelinas, deer, armadillo and, of course, hundreds of bird species. The main reason birders visit Aransas is to see the overwintering Whooping Cranes.

Even non-birders are at least vaguely aware of how close these magnificent birds came to extinction. In 1941 there were only fifteen or sixteen individuals known to be wintering in Texas. After more than fifty years of cooperative efforts by U.S. and Canadian wildlife personnel, there were 257 of them in 2001, including several captive flocks. If you saw the movie

*Fly Away Home* where a flock of Canada Geese was taught how to migrate by following ultra-light aircraft, you can imagine what that success did for teaching Whoopers how to get from their mostly Canadian breeding grounds back to their wintering grounds

Though we had seen a couple of Whooping Cranes a couple of years earlier at Bosque del Apache in New Mexico, we knew that neither of those birds survived the winter. It would be a treat to see some of the birds from the only viable migratory flock. It was with considerable excitement that we climbed up the observation tower at Aransas for our first search. Even with binoculars, the pair we first spotted was barely more than two very distant white specks in the brown marsh. For once we had brought along our spotting scope, and it was worth all the aggravation. With it we could make out details like the red marking that graces the tops of Whoopers' heads as well as the black face markings. Goosebumps were experienced. Enough said.

Besides the birds (which included both Brown and White Pelicans) we had our first encounter with a small group of javelinas. Javelinas are members of the group of mammals known as peccaries, or New World swine. Not to be confused with pigs, whose origins are traced to Afro-Eurasia,. even though they share cloven hooves and flat noses. I am not a mammal taxonomist, so I have no idea what subtle anatomical details distinguish the two groups. Plus I am too lazy to look them up. If they were bird families, I might bother...

At the visitor's center we got a stuffed javelin (toy! Not a taxidermist's project!) for our granddaughter, Sydney. We also got the first stamp in our Blue Goose Passport, a sort of souvenir book for visitors to National Wildlife Refuges. Can't say it ever caught on very big with us. We usually forgot to take it with us or found that many refuges didn't even have a stamper thingy.

After leaving Aransas NWR we headed south to Rockport. The level of air pollution spewing from various industrial sites on the coast was appalling. Of course, since it was all blowing out over the Gulf of Mexico, it really wasn't hurting anyone. Right? That was sarcasm in case you missed it. One of the legacies of Governor George W. Bush before he went on to share his environmental leadership with the rest of the country.

Along the way we got a wonderful look at another Caracara and two more White-tailed Kites. It turned out that White-tailed Kites used to be called Black-shouldered Kites. I decided they should be called White-tailed-black-shouldered-gray-backed-yellow-footed Kites so you wouldn't even have to look them up in the field guide.

Sunday, March 4, 2001 was my fifty-fifth birthday. We got up a little after 5 that morning. Checked out of the motel (after a "Continental Breakfast" of dishwater-strength coffee, orange juice and a Danish.) Drove back up to Aransas NWR and arrived there at dawn.

We got out of the car at the pond near the Visitor's Center and Sue immediately spotted a flock of Wild Turkeys in a tree. They made a lot of noise and flew down to the side of the road. The big Tom proceeded to regale his eight consorts with an impressive courtship display. What a treat! We wandered along the "Rail Trail" for a bit and found a Yellow-throated Warbler, a Hermit Thrush and numerous more common species. We found exactly zero rails. I counted them myself. At the Heron Flats observation area we did see a Clapper Rail – evidently he hadn't read the field guide, because he was walking along out in plain sight. Those guys are supposed to be secretive.

At Dagger Point we were able to ID an Eared Grebe out on the bay. At Hog Lake (which was more like Hog Large Mud Puddle) we saw a herd of White-tailed Deer, several Javelinas, a Lincoln's Sparrow and a couple of Brown Thrashers. We returned to the big observation tower for a last look at the Whooping Cranes in residence there and then left reluctantly to head for San Antonio.

I decided I needed to see 55 Kestrels in honor of my 55th birthday. We started seeing so many along the road that Sue suggested we needed 55 before lunch! We stopped at Beeville for sandwiches and decided to have a picnic at Choke Canyon State Park. We tallied 57 Kestrels just before we turned off I-37 for Choke Canyon.

Once in a while we stumble on a wonderful birding spot by accident. Choke Canyon State Park was just a dot on the map, but it was on our way to San Antonio, and it was close to lunch time. We pulled in and learned it would cost us six bucks to enter the park. Hmm. Might as well. Little did we know that the park was considered one of the best hot spots for birders in that part of Texas. We got 3 lifers during our lunch break: Golden-fronted Woodpecker, Summer Tanager and Cave Swallows! Plus one Roadrunner and more usual stuff. Our Texas list topped 80 there.

On to San Antonio where we checked into the Travelodge around 2:45. Walked over to see the Alamo. In one of our continuing series of happy coincidences, it was Alamo Weekend because the mission fell to its attackers on March 6, 1836. There were re-enactors dressed in frontier outfits and Mexican Army uniforms. It was worth seeing and I bought my mandatory kitsch – an Alamo thimble. Definitely tacky. We strolled along the Riverwalk and Sue bought me birthday dinner at the Presidio. She had pork medallions and I had calamari. For dessert she had chocolate cake and I had coconut and lime sorbets. While we were sitting outside eating, a bunch of White-winged Doves flew in – a lifer the easy way. Maybe we need a new hobby – Birding While Sitting at

42

Restaurants. We also saw a Brown-headed Cowbird which was new for our Texas list.

We slept in until nearly 7 the next morning. Had a big breakfast at the diner at the Travelodge, then went for a walk downtown. Checked out numerous shops but didn't find much we couldn't live without. I did buy a new cowboy hat and a small carving of a Roadrunner for my kitsch collection.

We decided to drive out to the Hill Country. Stopped at a small nature reserve in Boerne and picked up Lesser Goldfinches and Inca Doves among more common birds. There were also a number of Muscovy Ducks on the river in town. No doubt a flock of feral escapees. We counted them 'cause it's our list.

On the way back to San Antonio we had lunch at a Schlotzky's – good sandwiches. Then we stopped at Shepler's and I bought a pair of cowboy boots. I had to. The place was redolent of leather and it went to my head.

Went back to the motel and rested for an hour or so. Then we walked downtown and checked out The History Shop which was not that impressive. Took the riverboat tour of town for a pleasant half-hour ride. Had dinner at an overpriced Chinese restaurant on the Riverwalk. I ordered duck. That was what I got. No vegetables. No garnish. Just duck.

We got up early-ish Tuesday and had breakfast again at the Travelodge Diner. Checked out and headed out to Attwater Prairie Chicken NWR. We got there about 9:30 and stopped at the Visitor's Center. It turned out that no one was allowed near the Prairie Chickens except for the 1st weekend in April. Nuts. We drove around the auto route and saw some Cinnamon Teal (beautiful) and two lifers: Sprague's Pipit and a White-tailed Hawk. I started to walk part of the Sycamore Trail, but it was very wet and muddy so I gave up.

43

Sue drove from there to Houston – we stopped for Texas barbecue at lunch time. We got to the airport about 1:30 and took a room at the Quality Inn. Called a former colleague, Paul, who lived nearby, and he said he'd pick us up and take us to dinner. We returned our rental car while waiting and walked back to the motel. Paul took us to Papa's Seafood Restaurant. Then it was time to pack for the return trip to Philadelphia.

# Chapter 6
## Ohio, Indiana, Illinois – Birding at 65 (miles per hour)
## Friday, March 6 – Sunday, March 8, 1998

Sue's sister, Paula, and brother-in-law, Rick, lived in Evanston, Illinois during our quest. One of the consequences of this was that we made numerous trips from our home near Philadelphia out to their home north of Chicago. This, of course, necessitated driving across Ohio and Indiana to get there. When we had a bit of extra time we would supplement our "on the road" lists with stops at various birding hot spots. There were also several favorite places in and around Evanston where we eventually found more than fifty species for our Illinois list.

In March of 1998, for example, Sue's nephew was getting married and we planned to drive out to attend the wedding. Friday I took a personal day at work and we started out for Chicago. Drove all the way to the Indiana Dunes and checked them out a little - had an Eastern Screech Owl fly low in front of the car at dusk. Saturday we got up early and went birding around the dunes area. Got about thirty of our Indiana birds, including a Red-headed Woodpecker and a flock of Common Redpolls. The Redpolls were a lifer for Sue.

We drove to Chicago and arrived at Paula and Rick's in time for lunch. Checked into the Holiday Inn and took a nap before getting ready for the wedding.

The wedding itself was creative and beautiful. Sean built a stunning candelabra (for want of a better word) of strips of copper sheeting. The bride and groom were both of an artistic bent, and the entire ceremony and reception reflected their personalities. It was refreshingly unique. Plus we didn't have to do the stupid Chicken Dance.

Sunday the weather in Chicago turned nasty. Heavy rains and high winds. In order to get out of the house for a while (and away from people) we drove to the south side and looked for the rumored colony of Monk Parakeets. We located four nests, but the parakeets were smarter than we were and did not come out of them. We had dinner and conversation for several hours chez Shaffers, then went to bed early at the Holiday Inn.

Getting up reasonably early on Monday, we started home around 6:30 in the beginnings of a blizzard. Beginnings, hell. It was already a full-blown storm before we hit the road. The wind was trying to push Lake Michigan over onto Lakeshore Drive. Either that or the lake had some shopping it wanted to do in downtown Chicago.

Snow covered all the road signs and made them unreadable. This condition caused us an approximately twelve-mile detour down Route 394 to Chicago Heights. It took us more than five hours to cover the first 100 miles of our trip. Along the way, especially in the Gary, Indiana neighborhood, we saw numerous vehicles stranded off the pavement, including a number of semis that had tipped over into the median. There must have been at least a fifteen-mile backup on the westbound side around Gary. What an incredible mess.

The weather gradually improved as we moved east, and we made it to the vicinity of Youngstown, Ohio before quitting for the day. Exhausted, we checked into the only motel we could find near the Interstate. We have mercifully forgotten the name of the place. It was not a member of one of the major chains. It was grubby and dirty and tacky. It remains at the bottom of the scale of places we have stayed after many years of travel. That alone is pretty impressive. We were too exhausted to care, and certainly well beyond being able to find an alternative.

The next morning we got up later than usual, but hoped to get out of the motel as quickly as possible. When we got our stuff together and prepared to leave, we found that the storm had frozen the doors shut on our car. By the time we got them to open, we did not get on the road until about 7:30. Once we got rolling, though, we made good time, and got home around 2 p.m. even with stops for breakfast and a few groceries.

## Wednesday, May 23 – Tuesday, May 29, 2001

For our subsequent visit to Sue's family in Evanston, we planned to bird along the way and try to knock Ohio, Indiana and Illinois off our 50-bird lists. Our Illinois list was already at 47, so there was an excellent chance to finish that one. Ohio was only at 22 and Indiana at 33. We thought we should have a good shot at Ohio if we stopped at Ottawa NWR. Time might become a factor for Indiana.

The Ottawa National Wildlife Refuge was mostly wetlands set aside from remnants of the Great Black Swamp, an area in the heart of the Lake Erie Marsh Region. It was billed as offering the highest numbers of Bald Eagles in Ohio, and yes, we saw them on two separate visits. We only hiked a couple of miles of the seven and a half miles of trails. It was easy walking, because the refuge is all in the Lake Erie floodplain. Flat. Flat. Flat. To give an idea of how much the refuge means to the birds, Ottawa was voted by the readers of *Birder's World* as being among the Top 15 birding hotspots in America. It has also been named as a "site of regional significance" in the Western Hemisphere Shorebird Network. Plus it is designated an Important Bird Area by the American Bird Conservancy. We managed to get our fiftieth Ohio bird and a few extras, but we didn't really have time to savor Ottawa's promised diversity. Maybe next time.

We had made time for a stop at the Indiana Dunes National Seashore again before continuing on to Chicago. Despite the proximity to depressing and toxic industrial sites like Gary, the Indiana Dunes contained a wide range of habitats and consequently wonderful biodiversity. More than 350 species of birds had been recorded in the park, so it seemed likely we could get our goal of fifty pretty easily.

The park included about fifteen miles or so of Lake Michigan shoreline. Just inland from the edge of the lake were the dunes which give the park its name. Some of them rose as high as two hundred feet! Other habitats within the park included various kinds of wetlands nestled among the dunes as well as prairie remnants and forest fragments. In the course of our wandering, we managed to identify thirty-one species and bring our Indiana total to 61. Another state could be crossed off our list.

On Saturday, Paula and Rick took us up to the Chicago Botanic Gardens north of Evanston. Of course, Chicago is South of Evanston, but still. The Gardens themselves were beautifully laid out and checkered with pockets of very diverse habitat. This made it a good place to look for birds from the Japanese Garden to the Native Plant Garden. There was a Bonsai Collection which is NOT to be confused with the Dwarf Conifer Garden. So there! An English Oak Meadow was complemented by an English Walled Garden. There was an Aquatic Garden as well as a Water Garden. I'm not clear what the difference was there. Hmm. In any case, it was a lovely place to stroll around, and birds were all over the place.

So, the trip out to Evanston was a big success. We managed to get our fiftieth birds in Ohio (Brown-headed Cowbird), Indiana (Chipping Sparrow), and Illinois (House finch). We also got to see a ballgame at Wrigley Field – the Cubbies beat the Brewers 4-1.

Sammy Sosa went two for four with two singles. The weather was chilly, but pleasant.

On Monday Paula and Rick had a family cookout. Sean and Franny and the kids were there. We drove straight home on Tuesday, and it took nearly thirteen hours.

# Chapter 7
## Return to New Mexico and first trip to Arizona
## Saturday, March 2 – Friday, March 8, 2002

This was the first trip we took with our friend, J.T. He was an English professor at the university where I taught and had gone to Oxford, England with us as part of a program that Sue and I ran during the summers. He was dreading retirement because he didn't have anything to do. We introduced him to birding and eventually invited him to join our quest. J.T. was a big man, both tall and wide. He had bad hips that needed to be replaced. He was the baby of his family and had been spoiled by his big sisters. We were warned by colleagues that he had a notorious temper, but we only knew his sweet and gracious side. We also knew that no matter how hard he tried, he would never be a good birder. He enjoyed having us find and identify birds for him, but on his own he was pretty shaky on both counts.

"Cereal and coffee?"

"Sounds good.," It was only two AM and we had a long day ahead of us. While having our light breakfast a pair of Great Horned Owls hooted a duet behind the house. We stepped out onto the deck and spotted them in our big oak tree. Silhouetted against a brightly moonlit sky, they continued their singing as we watched. A good omen from the Gods of Birding.

We picked up J.T. around 3:30 and he drove us all to the Philadelphia airport. Getting there by 4:15 or so, we got through security fairly smoothly. This was the spring following the 9/11 attacks and the first time we had to remove our shoes. Our spotting scope raised some questions with the guards until Sue took it out and demonstrated that one could, in fact, look through it. No hidden explosives. Maybe a bit of dust on the lens, but nothing threatening.

The layover in St. Louis gave us time to grab a bite to eat. I enjoyed a hot dog that was slightly warmer than my body temperature and cost four bucks. J.T. suggested I could have stuck one up my ass to keep it warm from home and saved some money. That image became a recurring theme on the trip. No further comment needed.

The flight from St. Louis to Albuquerque was uneventful. This is always a positive thing. After collecting our luggage we picked up our rental car at the Dollar counter.

Sue drove to El Malpais National Conservation Area. The landscape was pretty stark, having been formed by ancient volcanic activity. We hiked a bit round the lava flows and cinder cones and surprisingly got several good birds – at least a couple of lifers for each of us. OK, since you ask, the Prairie Falcon was definitely a lifer for all three of us, and I'm pretty certain the Sage Thrasher was, too. We didn't have a lot of time to spare there, so we pressed on to Arizona.

We reached the Painted Desert at 5:20 PM only to find it had closed at 5. Nuts. So we continued on to Holbrook, where we spent the night at the Best Western. While J.T. and I were registering and yukking it up with the clerk, Sue found a Black-throated Sparrow in the parking lot. I never did locate it. We did find a Cassin's Finch, but I was insanely jealous of the sparrow.

We got up early and had a big breakfast before driving over to the Painted Desert/Petrified Forest. The park opened at 8, and we got there a few minutes early. While waiting for the gate to open, we spotted and got great looks at three Townsend's Solitaires.

Once inside the actual park, we were treated to multi-colored vistas that slowly evolved as the angle of the sun changed. We took a lot of photographs, but as is often the case, the grandeur of the scene simply defied capture.

I was impressed by the quantity of petrified wood in the Petrified Forest where Sue took numerous pictures of J.T. and me among the stone trunks. Then we went to the Homol'ovi Ruins State Park. Saw a number of Say's Phoebes, a juvenile Golden Eagle being harassed by Ravens and a small flock of White-crowned Sparrows plus a bunch of Horned Larks. John assured us that the ruins were charged with powerful spiritual energy, a phenomenon I am unable to detect.

Next I drove to Meteor Crater. It was much more than a big hole in the ground. Not that it *wasn't* a big hole in the ground. It was about four thousand feet across and more than five hundred feet deep. The visitor center and museum had educational exhibits about the crater that included some fragments of the meteorite that formed it. The largest piece found at that time was around fourteen hundred pounds. They also had an Astronaut Hall of Fame and information about other impacts on the earth and other planets. I loved it.

At Sunset Crater we learned that the last major eruption was "only" about a thousand years ago. Maybe as little as nine hundred. Like many such blasted landscapes, it was comforting to see the multiple ways life had reasserted itself. Wildflowers, trees, and small critters further up the food chain suggest the ecology had already achieved a complex level of development.

Wupatki was one of those wonderful places that inspired one to reflect on history and the ephemeral quality of human endeavors. The ruins suggested a population of several thousand puebloan ancestors once called the place home. All have dispersed now, although contemporary Hopi and Navajo people still treat the site as sacred.

There must have been a couple of thousand American Robins flocking at Wupatki, probably

because there was a modest lake (more like a large pond) in the midst of the desert. We also saw several little gray ground squirrels and a herd of five pronghorns there. Unfortunately, I didn't note any field marks for the squirrels, so I was unable to identify the species later. We had lunch at a three-calendar diner[3] on Route 66 in Winslow. We had Mexican food, because we could. My tacos were delicious. That evening we stayed at Cameron in a beautiful room. We had dinner at the Trading Post and I bought myself a new cowboy hat.

Another birthday arrived for me while birding in the West. We got up around 5 so we could get to the Grand Canyon at sunrise. Wow. Spectacular. Indescribable. At the Desert View overlook we watched as the light began illuminating the tops of the rock formations.

There were several Ravens loitering around the parking lot and I had a conversation with one. He spoke only body language, but we understood one another. At one point, for example, he clearly said, "One step closer and I'm out of here, Buster."

We stopped at a number of scenic view spots. At one there were four young people who needed to be killed, but we didn't. The way they were capering about on rocks at the rim of the canyon, there was a good chance gravity would take them out of the gene pool. We just moved on – after spotting a Juniper Titmouse, of course. As the morning wore on, the shadows in the Canyon looked bluer and bluer – a deep incredible blue. Never saw the likes anywhere else.

We had a huge breakfast at El Tovar – J.T. and I had the "Navajo Taco" which included blackened beef, potatoes, roasted peppers, onions and salsa served on Navajo fry bread. As a former farm boy, I was dismayed

---

[3] See *Blue Highways* by William Least Heat-Moon if you want to know what a three-calendar diner is.

when I couldn't actually eat it all! We tried to find some birds for a while but they were sparse and J.T. was tired so we drove down to Flagstaff. Checked into a Best Western Motel (the Pony Soldier) and took a nap. Then went for a brief walk at Thorp Park. Found our first American Crows for Arizona and three Pygmy Nuthatches. Also saw an Abert's Squirrel (identified after we got back) – my notes described it as "a Fox? Squirrel? Reddish on back with big furry ears." There was a "Doggy Park" across from Thorp – a large fenced-in area with dozens of dogs and people enjoying the space. We thought it was a pretty cool idea. Dinner was at the Weatherford Hotel – atmosphere from the early 1900s and good food.

After a big breakfast at Kathy's Café in Flagstaff, we drove down through Oak Creek Canyon and Sedona all the way to Montezuma's Castle. There we finally had some decent birding. Also stopped at Montezuma's Well and got some more birds. Had lunch at the Hideaway Restaurant in Sedona and continued back through Oak Creek Canyon to Slide Rock State Park. Sue and I PROBABLY saw an American Dipper at Slide Rock, but we were not certain enough to actually count it. Back to Flagstaff for the evening. The plan for the next day was to head back to New Mexico and show J.T. around Bosque del Apache .

The following morning we ate breakfast again at Kathy's Café because we had enjoyed it the previous day. Not just the food, but the cultural experience. Kathy was one of those too-thin, stuck-in-the-sixties women who dressed in long skirts and hiking boots, had a ring in her nose, and ate no meat nor watched any TV. She had four daughters (she showed us a picture) named Maya, Déjà, and two others that end in "a" – possibly Pellagra and Viagra, but we can't remember. She also had a large dog named "VW." She served a hearty breakfast and played music appropriate to the setting – that morning it was a local band that will remain just that if our assessment means anything (which it probably doesn't.)

We headed for Lyman Lake State Park with a faint hope of getting our last few Arizona birds . It turned out that Sue ended up with 51 and I had 49. Probably because I slept through a number of Red-tailed Hawks while napping in the back seat. We were planning to go back some summer for the hummingbirds anyway. We got a few birds at Lyman Lake, but it was not as busy as we expected for a body of water out in the desert.

After Lyman, we headed southeast toward Bosque del Apache. Stopped in Springerville and had burgers and fries at Booga Red's. I wasn't sure it wasn't Boogar Ed's, but the sign must have been correct. We saw a herd of Pronghorns near the VLA. Stopped at Water Canyon and got a few birds (best was a colony of Acorn Woodpeckers working at their stash in a dead tree.) Checked into a motel in Socorro and proceeded to Bosque. Bosque lived up to its reputation, yielding about 32 species in 1½ hours or so. J.T. got several lifers including the Sandhill Cranes.

Thursday morning we arrived at Bosque before 7 and the birding was intense for about two hours. We got about 50 birds including one "mystery bird." We were inching along the access road when we spotted a brownish speckly bird with an enormously long tail perched in a tree. We stopped and rolled down the windows and it was making quiet calls sort of like a cuckoo. We were intrigued. Then it finally flew down and scampered away. On the ground we immediately recognized it as a Greater Roadrunner. Somehow seeing it in a TREE had us completely bamboozled. Other highlights for the morning included Cinnamon Teal, Black-crowned Night-herons, Gambel's Quail, Bald Eagles, one Avocet, and Yellow-headed Blackbirds. The dust conditions were awful, so Sue decided to stay in Socorro this afternoon. J.T. and I went back to Bosque and it was very windy, but we got a great look at a flock of Sandhill Cranes.

## GUSTY WINDS MAY EXIST

They sure as hell did that Friday. We drove up to Albuquerque from Socorro and as we approached the city, it was completely shrouded in swirling clouds of dust. We drove out to the Rio Grande Nature Center and found 33 species in about an hour and a half. Checked into our motel around 11:30 and ate a light lunch. Then slept and read for a while – Sue went out to do some shopping. When I went into the bathroom, I swear the wind was raising whitecaps *in the toilet!*

Sue and I wandered around the shops in the Old Town for an hour or so. Bought a matted print of an Indian design in deep reds and blacks. Went back and got J.T. for dinner at Scala. It was as good as we remembered from our last visit. J.T. and I had the pasta special – duck and gorgonzola wrapped in a pasta shells. Sue had pumpkin-stuffed ravioli that she pronounced "very good." The bookstore we had planned to visit was closed after we ate, so we returned to the motel. We flew home the next morning.

# Chapter 8
## New Mexico and Arizona, Again?
### January 9 – 13, 2003

On Saturday morning we decided to make a stop at the Rio Grande Nature Center in northwestern Albuquerque rather than waste prime birding time driving down to Bosque del Apache. We saw about twenty species, including Sandhill Cranes and the usual wonderful looks at Wood Ducks. While there we ran into a fellow who was about to lead a nature walk, and he asked whether we knew about the Rosy Finches at Sandia Crest. Of course we didn't. So he gave us directions (which Sue remembered most of and I remembered a little of – but that's another story) and after about an hour we headed up the mountain. At the crest was a visitor's center with numerous bird feeders and we saw several Steller's Jays, many Cassin's Finches, and yes, two out of three of the Rosy Finches. We may have even seen all three Rosy Finches, but they were sort of confusing and we had no experience seeing any of them before. Two lifers was a good morning in any case. We stopped at the ski area in hopes of a glimpse of a rumored Northern Pygmy Owl, but saw nothing there.

On to Bosque, where we saw about twenty-five birds or so. Most impressive to Sue and me was the American Dipper who gave us a looooong look. My pictures of him, unfortunately, show a vague gray blob in the middle of heavy vegetation. Oh well, a lifer is a lifer.

On Sunday we had an early breakfast (at about 6.) Sue and I got down to Bosque del Apache right around sunrise. We had a wonderful morning of birding there as always. Sue wanted to check out the Canyon Trail, so we did that and saw a flock of Verdins and another life bird, Brewer's Sparrows. I was looking at them and thinking "these are strangely pale sparrows" and looked them up in my field guide to read that Brewer's Sparrows are "a pale sparrow with a blank expression." I missed the blank expression, but noted that they do live in desert scrub, which was where we were.

We drove to Magdalena for lunch at Evett's Café and it did not disappoint. This time there I took a picture of the "Thelma, Queen of Perfumes" sign and it came out very well, thank you. Then we drove back to Water Canyon, which had very few birds indeed. There were some very rough-looking characters out there hanging around in camping trailers. We decided discretion was the better part of valor, so we did not stay long. It was the middle of the day, and all we got was an Acorn Woodpecker and a Loggerhead Shrike. Hey, they were new for the day and the only ones we saw for the trip.

On the way back to Bosque we caught sight of a Turkey Vulture and a couple of Rock Doves (not normally exciting, but contributing to a new one-day high for January of 64 birds.[4])

Back at Bosque we continued around the access loops and picked up Black-tailed Gnatcatcher, Long-billed Dowitcher, and Pinyon Jay – all lifers for Sue and me.

Monday we decided to check out Sevilleta National Wildlife Refuge. Not much happening there except a gazillion Red-winged Blackbirds, a couple of hundred Robins and (new for the trip) some Cedar Waxwings.

We drove up to Santa Fe to look for a new turquoise ring for me. Did I mention that I lost my old ring at security in the Philadelphia Airport? Well, I found a beautiful (and expensive) ring at the first store we checked in Santa Fe and we had lunch at a burrito place while it was being resized.

---

[4] Yes. I keep a list of the best one-day totals for every month of the year.

Oops. I forgot we made a short stop at Petroglyph National Monument on our way north and found a flock of Scaled Quail there! One of their folk names is "Cotton Tops" because of the tuft of white feathers protruding from the tops of their heads. That was lifer number eight for the trip for Sue and me. Pretty damned impressive. After lunch we drove out to Bandelier to look for a Pygmy Nuthatch. Nothing much was happening at the visitor center except a lone Raven walking around the parking lot. On the way back out, however, we spotted a Townsend's Solitaire and a Juniper Titmouse. A pair of Black-billed Magpies on the way back to Albuquerque turned out to be species number 81 for the trip.

### Sunday, February 02, 2003 - Interlude
Sue and I were working on plans for our Arizona trip in May, and getting pretty psyched. We finally found rooms available at the Southwest Research Station in Portal for our three days' excursion to the Cave Creek/Chiricahua Mountain areas. Good thing we didn't wait much longer, because all the B&B places seemed to be already booked!

### Friday, May 9 – Tuesday, May 20, 2003
Tucson — Flew from Philly to Phoenix. Either I forgot to make a car reservation, or it wasn't with Alamo. Alamo rented us a car as a "walk in." We were driving a red Alero, which was a squeeze for J.T., but he'd be OK. We stopped briefly at Casa Grande National Monument. We had gotten somewhat lost because of vague maps and poorly-marked roads[5], so we got there about twenty minutes before they were going to close. The good news is they let us in free, because it was so late. The other good news is there wasn't all that much to see there anyway and we had saved the price of admission. We did see a small flock

---

[5] We still do not own a GPS. Where is the fun in those?

of Gambel's Quail and lots of Round-tailed Ground Squirrels (cute little buggers.)

That night we stayed in The Congress Hotel that had been preserved pretty much the same since John Dillinger was captured there in the 1930s. Or maybe the 1920s. You could look it up. I didn't. They had an old PBX Telephone Switchboard, a vintage radio in the room, old-fashioned fixtures in the bathroom and a period barbershop in the lobby.

We had a big breakfast at the Horseshoe Café in Benson, AZ the next morning. The waitress was from Columbus, OH, and was too perky for my taste. She talked too much and wouldn't let anyone change the TV channel from some crap that I have mercifully forgotten. Seems like it was something like MTV. That sort of drivel. She was friendly and all that, but annoying at that hour. Basta. We got to the Southwest Research Station a little after 10. By lunch time we had identified three hummingbirds that were new to us (Black-chinned, Blue-throated and Magnificent.) Lunch was black bean soup and salad. We got three meals a day there (total cost only $101 a day for **two** of us.) Our room was large – beds for 5, and we had a little "porch" – more accurately a concrete slab with chairs – in front. We birded for an hour or so at the South Fork and got Black-throated Gray Warbler, MacGillivray's Warbler [probably not, I decided not to count it] and a Plumbeous Vireo. I think I got about fourteen or fifteen life birds that day! That hadn't happened in a loooooooong time. We took naps that afternoon and I hiked up behind the station and didn't see too much.

Our first full day at Cave Creek. Lots of life birds. No Trogons, but we wandered around the Research Station before breakfast – I saw a Lark Sparrow and a Hooded Oriole before Sue came out. Best "before breakfast" bird was a Lazuli Bunting (which turned out to be my 400th North American bird.) Actually, we saw a pair of them. We were lucky to run into a "western" birder who told us what it was, or we would probably still be looking through our books for it! Jenna. Her name. Or possibly Janet. She was a strange bird in her own right. Late forties or early fifties, mousy brown hair and carrying a tad more weight than she needed to be healthy. She seemed to have some emotional issues about wildlife. For example, we seldom burst into tears when we come across a dead butterfly... She was pleasant and helpful in identifying all the strange birds that we didn't know, but she needed a long rest. Or something.

The Research Station was like a cross between a scout camp and a motel. We got three meals a day, which was a good thing since we were a loooooong way from any real town. Portal had a store, a café, a post office, a fire station and a handful of houses. Douglas was around sixty miles away. Before breakfast I took a GPS reading near our cabin: 31° 52.992 N; 109° 12.365 W, elevation 5408 feet.[6] I started to take a second reading and left the receiver on top of the car while talking to a couple from Michigan. I drove off with it still on top of the car and never saw it again. Alas. We went to the South Fork area looking for Trogons after breakfast. Neither heard nor seen. We still saw some nice birds. J.T. and I finally saw our Painted Buntings. We came back to the Station and rested until lunch.

We drove over to Portal and Sue and I walked a trail beyond the Post Office, managing to find a Cactus Wren, a Curve-billed Thrasher, a Great Horned Owl that Janet had told us about in a broken sycamore with honeycombs in the hollow part, and a flock of Lesser Goldfinches. We got sodas and snacks at the store, and while we sat outside, a Canyon Towhee flew in – just for J.T. He saw a Hepatic Tanager while we were hiking.  Sue and I got a nice look at a Broad-tailed

---

[6] Ok.ok. I did have a GPS , but not the kind that tells you to turn left at the next stop sign.

Hummingbird while there, too. Then we drove east from Portal to look for desert birds. Found Black-throated Sparrows for J.T. and me – you may recall that Sue saw one the last time we were out this way. There was a dirt lane called McAvoy Road, so we drove down it only to discover a trashy redneck domicile with its residents looking none-too-friendly, so I made a u-turn and we went on our way. Spotted several interesting mammals – Blacktailed Jackrabbit, Yuma Antelope Squirrel and a Yellow-nosed Cotton Rat. No, I didn't make that last one up! There were also several Cliff Chipmunks running around the campground. The Whip-poor-wills called loudly again that evening and Sue and I stayed up past 8 to look for them. Well, we heard at least two. Saw nearly one. We planned to leave at 5:30 in the morning in search of the elusive Trogons! One fellow said they were among the first birds to stir at dawn. We'd see.

J.T. and I left camp at 5:20 or so and drove to South Fork in search of Trogons. Sue decided to stay in bed. We drove slowly up the canyon, stopping every little way to listen. After only fifteen or twenty minutes, we heard a male calling to our left and upslope from us. Got out of the car and started towards the sound. It started moving up the canyon slowly but steadily. I kept walking until I realized I was passing the point where the call was currently coming from. I pulled up my binoculars and there he was – sitting out in the open! I waved to J.T. to hurry, and not only did the bird wait for him, it waited for another couple to park and walk up to join us. Wow. Drove back to the Research Station to get Sue, but on our return there was neither sound nor sight of a Trogon.

Then we drove to Douglas and gassed up the car and picked up stuff for lunch. Next on the itinerary was Chiricahua National Monument. Not much in the line of birds, but the rock formations were spectacular. We took the back way to return to Cave Creek – a long, rough, dirt road with the smoothest stretches being the cattle guards – stopping at Rustler's Park on top of a mountain. We did see a Western Tanager on the way.

Sunset in Cave Creek Canyon. Quiet. Peaceful. The rock face glows red and green. Sandstone and lichen. Silence descends broken by a few squabbling kingbirds and the comical squawks of acorn woodpeckers. A tiny deer grazes next to our cabin. Tired birders and researchers disperse to their respective cabins. As darkness deepens, cries of whip-poor-wills punctuate the silence. An enchanting moment in a magical place...

We started imagining a series of bird-related mystery novels today. I offered as the first title, *Verdin of Proof*. The author was initially to be Robin Becard, but I think it will have to be Jean-Luc... Might as well be totally silly. We can see the series continuing with titles like *Flicker of Hope*, *Hard to Swallow*, *Stork Reality*, *Wren for your Life*. You probably had to be there.

Sue and I set out ca. 5:20 the next morning in quest of the Elegant Trogon. We tried the area along South Fork with zero success. Sue wanted to check out the "waterfalls" on the other side of the Research Station. When we pulled into the camping area there was a retired couple there and the woman said we had missed a male Trogon by a couple of minutes. Sounds like *Endless Summer* – "aw, you guys shoulda been here yesterday!" At least Sue got to hear one call.

We spent the rest of the morning driving to Sierra Vista. We drove out to the Huachuca Military Reservation and birded in Garden Canyon. Sue and I found a Black-chinned Hummingbird on her nest and Sue got her Hepatic Tanager. We had lunch at a buffet place called the Golden Corral and checked into our motel at 2. Decided we were too tired to do anything else. Birded from the balcony – there were two male

Gambel's Quail sitting on the fence out back at one point.

We started the following day with breakfast at Mickey D's. There were two noteworthy things there: 1. A brochure from McDonald's giving nutritional advice. I did not make this up. 2. A cash machine for getting McMoney. I didn't make that up, either! Ah, pop culture. Or capitalism. Whatever.

Decided to check out San Pedro National Conservation Something-or-other. Drove down past Ramsey Canyon and realized we were going the wrong way. Stopped for directions at the Lone Star Café on Rte. 92. We still got to San Pedro shortly after seven, and the birding was wonderful. Within a few minutes we found Green-tailed Towhees and Vermilion Flycatchers! Sue and I hiked the loop trail and got lots of good stuff, including a Zone-tailed Hawk. I'm not positive, but that may be the only bird on our life lists that begins with a "Z". There were lots of little lizards running along the trail that I later identified as Desert Grassland Whiptails.

We stopped for an hour or so at Ramsey Canyon. By that time (10:30 or so) the birding there was pretty lame and we were hot and tired. We decided to return to the Lone Star Café for lunch. Talk about local characters! Well, sort of local. The waitress, Crystal, was from Allentown, PA, about an hour and a half from where we lived. She was much too loud and perky for my taste (there seems to be a lot of that in Arizona) – but certainly friendly. She said she was in love with the area, and had lived all over the country. She confessed she had never spent July and August there, though. The cook was a skinny, thirty-something guy with black hair in a ponytail in a hairnet and with at least four or five missing teeth. He was very proud of his meatloaf special, which he pronounced "delicious." I am sorry to say we didn't try it. We went back to our room to escape the midday heat. We were exhausted. Sue was nursing a nasty migraine headache. J.T. and I had supper at Schlotzky's again. I won a pizza as part of some promotion they were running. I gave it to a soldier who was stationed at Fort Huachuca.

We got going a little before 6 and had breakfast at Mickey D's again. I got $100 from the McMoney Machine. Sue's headache was not better, so she stayed at the motel while J.T. and I went to San Pedro for a couple of hours. The birding was outstanding again – numerous Vermilion Flycatchers and we got a nice look at a Black-bellied Whistling Duck. Returned to the motel circa 9 and headed for Tucson.

Sue suggested stopping at Saguaro National Park, and it was really magical. The vegetation was mostly cacti, Palo Verde and Mesquite. Despite being midday, we saw quite a few interesting birds. We found a nest with a pair of Black-tailed Gnatcatchers fighting off an assault by a Cactus Wren. Several Gila Woodpeckers and one Gilded Flicker.

From there Sue drove to Phoenix – had lunch at an authentic Mexican place along the way. We checked in at a Sleep Inn near the airport. J.T. was leaving for Philly in the morning. We were a little vague at the moment about what to do for our last three days. Something north of there, in any case. The temperatures were expected to be around 100° all week. It would be twenty degrees cooler north of Flagstaff.

We grabbed breakfast at our motel at 6 the next morning and drove to Flagstaff via Wilcox – seeing some pretty country along the way. We checked into a Red Roof Inn just off I-40 and Sue called a local pharmacy who agreed to contact Eckert's back home and fill her Imitrex prescription. She was finally feeling better. After we picked up the medicine, we drove out to Walnut Canyon and walked the trail around the cliff dwellings. Strenuous but worthwhile. Saw a few birds along the way, including a Purple Martin and a Black-headed Grosbeak. The next day we planned to drive up to the Grand Canyon in hopes of finding a California Condor.

After breakfast the following day at 6 at the Cracker Barrel next door to our motel, we drove up to the Grand Canyon. We stopped at Red Mountain Trail about half way to the canyon and hiked back into the cinder cone. We did this around 8, when it was still cool. The scenery was really spectacular and we had the bonus of spotting a Raven's nest and a Prairie Falcon nest in holes in the cliffs. The female falcon was seated on a ledge while the male flew acrobatic loops and swoops in an evident effort to impress her. She did not move, whether from fascination or boredom it was impossible for mere humans to say.

At the Grand Canyon we hiked from Bright Angel Lodge to Yavapai Observation Point and saw nearly one Condor. We did spot a few other birds, and got good looks at a Black-throated Gray Warbler and a Western Tanager.

On the way back to the motel we spent an hour or so at the Museum of Northern Arizona. They had an interesting and eclectic collection of fossils and artifacts, and we bought an owl sculpture by a local artist.

We drove up to the Vermilion Cliffs in hopes of spotting a California Condor. No luck on that front, but we saw a lot of spectacular scenery. I am overusing "spectacular" but cannot think of another word at the moment. Memorable seems too tame. Pretty and beautiful seem too bland. I give up. [It was more than seven years later – in September 2010 that we finally found a couple of Condors.]

We drove all the way into Utah and back across to Lake Powell. Got a couple of Ravens and a Western Kingbird in Utah. Only forty-eight to go for Utah. We stopped for lunch in Page, AZ and ate at a little

66

Mexican place called Zapata's. The food was both authentic and delicious. On the way back down to Flagstaff, we stopped at a Navajo roadside stand and Sue bought a beautiful rug.

Started the day with a big breakfast at Cathy's Café. She was as retro as ever. Her dress that day was low-cut in the back and we got to see her enormous tattoo – a tree of some kind. She broke a foot the night before sliding down a rock with friends. She gave us directions to Mormon Lake which we promptly muddled and missed our turn.

So we took 89A through Oak Creek Canyon and went to Tuzigoot National Monument. The pueblo ruins were interesting, but we also birded along the river and got not one, but FOUR Phainopeplas! (Turned out to be Sue's 400th North American Bird.) Numerous lizards along the trail, including some whiptails, a fattish fellow with a red-orangeish head, one of the tiny guys with black and white undertail, a bluish collared guy (I think it was a Collared Lizard, duh.) Another with a black collar and checkered back of brown-green-yellowish pattern. Might be the same guy.

# Chapter 9
## Rhode Island and a Start on Connecticut
### Friday, November 8 – Monday, November 11, 2002

Sue left work at noon on Friday and we drove up the Northeast Extension [PA Turnpike] to Quakertown. Then we took some back roads around Allentown and hooked up with I-78 near Easton. Along the way we saw a flock of Wild Turkeys. Pretty cool. We took I-78 to I-287 and took it up to near Suffern, NY where we swung around to the Tappan Zee Bridge. Cut across to I-95 east of New York and headed across Connecticut on the Merrit Parkway. We hit Connecticut right around rush hour, and took nearly two hours to cover the next forty miles. The Parkway was lined with mature trees and punctuated by a series of overpasses. Each bridge had individual character – some were broad single arches, some double arches, some were all concrete, others stone. A couple of them had crenellations while most were plain. One bridge had a distinctive downward slant from left to right. Another rose slightly the opposite way. It was all a sharp contrast with I-95 and its lack of trees and cookie-cutter bridges, all with straight (and rusty) steel beam and concrete construction. Of course, the traffic was a lot heavier on I-95, if you like stress. We found a motel in Saybrook and spent the night.

Saturday morning we birded our way along the Connecticut and Rhode Island coasts with stops at Saybrook, Rocky Neck State Park, Stonington and the Stewart McKinney NWR. Managed to find 35 species in Connecticut, and nearly as many in Rhode Island before deciding it was time to find a place for the night. We wound up in Narragansett. Found a local "pub" for dinner and fell asleep very early.

On Sunday we got up around 5:30 and started out looking for breakfast. Along the way we discovered metropolitan Perryville, RI. A town of at least a couple of hundred souls. One church. One very tacky-looking garage. Clean and neat at one end, grubby and tatty at the other. The town. Not the garage. The garage was all grubby and tatty. This grand metropolitan area had no fewer than THREE exits from Route 1. We ate at a coffee and bake shop off Route 1. The food was mediocre, but we were hungry. We learned that it was a place "cooking for Christ." All of the tables were decorated with Bible quotes, as were the water bottles, coffee cups, napkins and walls. "Christ is the Answer." I couldn't help wondering what the question was. "For I am the LORD. I change not. – Malachi 3:6." Plus a couple of quotes from Matthew. You get the idea. I got the creeps.

After breakfast, we headed for Trustom Pond NWR. The "pond" itself was billed by the National Wildlife Refuge system as Rhode Island's only undeveloped salt pond. The refuge encompassed a variety of habitats from forest to barrier beach. The birding was wonderful and before we were finished there we had 53 species for Rhode Island! Highlights were two Brown Creepers, a Eurasian Wigeon, several Northern Gannets, a Great Cormorant and a nice look at two River Otters. Yes, I know that River Otters are mammals.

We met a couple of volunteers who chatted with us about birds and birding for about twenty minutes. The woman, Kimberly, had family in our area, and we invited them to give us a call if they got down this way. Of course, that assumed they could remember our names. Um, no, they never did.

We started for home about 9:20 in the morning and got there by a rather circuitous route a little before 5.

Pooped, but happy.

## Chapter 10
## The Gulf Coast
## Saturday, March 1 – Saturday, March 8, 2003

We got up a little after 3 and had some breakfast. Left the house around 4 and picked up J.T. Got to the airport by about 5 and our flight was scheduled to leave at 7:30, but we didn't leave until about 8. God, this is getting as boring as the trip was. We had about a one hour layover in Charlotte, NC and left late for Pensacola.

We landed in Pensacola about noon and picked up our car at Alamo. Drove down to Santa Rosa Island and had some trouble finding a room. Finally got rooms at $130 a night plus tax. Turned out to cost $148. Ouch. We ate lunch at the hotel restaurant and then drove over to Gulf Islands National Seashore. In the course of our wanderings we identified 28 birds, including a Loggerhead Shrike, an American Kestrel, a couple of Ruddy Turnstones. Along the nature trail we had an encounter with an armadillo. What a curious creature he was! He didn't seem too concerned about our presence, snuffling about with his snout poking into the sand looking for grubs. Looked a bit like a gray dachshund wearing a suit of leather armor. Neither Sue nor I had seen one before. J.T., the Okie-boy, grew up with them, of course.

Sunday we put in a loooooong day today following a mediocre night's sleep. We stayed at the Beachside Inn in Gulf Breeze, FL Saturday night, south of Pensacola. There were a few Mardi Gras revelers staying there as well, including two Leather-lunged Drunks, a pair of birds we didn't need on our life lists.

We got up a little after 5 that morning and got going just about 6. Breakfast at Mickey D's. Then we headed to Alabama to get our fifty birds. We had maps of the Alabama Coastal Birding Trail, so we thought we'd hit the best-looking spots.

Stop number one (Perdido Pass/Alabama Point-East) featured lots of Brown Pelicans, Double-crested Cormorants, several Great Blue Herons, a couple of Tree Swallows and some Sanderlings. A pretty nice start in terms of quality, although we only got ten species.

On to site #3 on our map – Boggy Point – where we got a nice variety, including a Brown Thrasher, a flock of Cedar Waxwings, an Eastern Bluebird, a Fish Crow, two Great Egrets, a Catbird and an Osprey. Sixteen species at that stop.

Stop #5 on the birding trail was at Gulf State Park Campground where we got a Eurasian Collared Dove, a nice look at an Eastern Towhee, a Cattle Egret and our first Barn Swallow for the year. Unfortunately, the only other bird we managed to find there was an American Robin. A five-species stop.

We were not getting very many species at each stop, but the varied habitats were at least yielding different ones. Ten here, sixteen there, another fourteen on the road and before you know it you have forty species. We hoped our last couple of places would produce the other ten that we needed.

We drove out to catch the ferry to Dauphin Island, but when we got all the way out there, the ferry was "in dry dock until Thursday."

"We sure wish it was runnin' fer ya," says Bubba. Despite his wishes, we had to drive all the way back to and completely around Mobile Bay.

Stopped for lunch at a place called The Hitchin' Post. For the second day in a row I decided to sample the local crawfish Po Boy. Like the one the previous night, I would describe this one as deconstructed. Yesterday's in Florida had a tastier sauce. Both were served on two separate pieces of bread with fried crawfish on one, lettuce, tomato and onion (today's only) on the other piece. Sauce in one of those little plastic cups on the side. Oh, I almost forgot! Today's appetizer was a large plate of batter-fried – are you ready for this? – dill pickle chips. I am NOT making this up. Our waitress, Tammy, was a 40-ish skinny, weak-chinned, bleached blonde with a drawl you could cut with a knife. When I used the restroom there was a bright red plastic cigarette butt catcher in the urinal that warned, "Say No to Drugs!" I know I was inspired.

We birded at Bon Secour NWR where a longish hike yielded some good birds. Made brief stops at Week's Bay and Fairhope and picked up a couple of insurance birds. On the way we saw a Loggerhead Shrike and - ta dah – a MISSISSIPPI KITE. Lifer! Lifer! Total for the day seemed to be about 51 or 52 [It turned out to be 53 for Sue, 54 for Jim. Sue missed the Coot along the road.] Another state crossed off our list.

We started out at about 6 from Moss Point, MS and got about nine birds around the Cracker Barrel where we had breakfast. First stop was Grand Bay NWR which was new and largely undeveloped. By the time we left we had over 20 birds and a great start. Highlight was a female Prothonotary Warbler and a handful of White-throated Sparrows. On the road we passed a billboard put up by the Seventh-Day Adventists that declared:

## Saturday, the Lord's Day – Sunday the Anti-Christ

Gosh, we didn't know that! Later we passed a church camp or some such place with a sign out front that read, "Kickin' it for Christ! The beginning of the youth explosion!" Was it a soccer camp? Baptist thugs? God only knows. On to Ward Bayou, where we got Black Vultures, a Brown Thrasher, an Orange-crowned Warbler and lots of Eastern Bluebirds. At Davis Bayou a Kingfisher, some more Tree Swallows and several Hooded Mergansers. Also two Yellow-bellied Sapsuckers. We drove around the Mississippi Sandhill

Crane NWR and didn't find squat. We finally hit our fiftieth MS bird at the Pass Christian and Waveland area where we saw more than 100 Black Skimmers, a flock of Ruddy Turnstones, a few Bufflehead and 2 Greater Scaup.

Mardi Gras, March 4, 2003. Oh, yeah, and my 57th birthday. Started the day in Covington, LA. We got our usual early start and drove out to Whiskey Bay Rd. to explore the Atchafalaya NWR and associated Wildlife Management Area. Total miles out from Covington was about 115. Whiskey Bay Road was unpaved and about 20 miles long. We know, because when we got almost to the north end, a road crew had sealed off the final mile to work on a railroad crossing, and we had to return 18 miles to get back to I-10. On the way north we got a wonderful look at a Hermit Thrush. We started to feel like we were in a space-time warp from a cheap sci-fi flick. Endless levee on the left, endless swamp on the right. On the return, of course, the swamp and levee switched sides. We got a reasonable assortment of birds, including 3 or 4 Pileated Woodpeckers, four Red-shouldered Hawks, and a few Black Vultures.

On the way back to Covington we ate at a Shoney's. I had a turkey club (good idea) and fried onion rings (bad idea.) The onion rings haunted me all afternoon. Yuck. I didn't even feel like having any dinner. After we checked into our motel, we drove over to Fontainebleau State Park to check it out. While there we added six species to our Louisiana list, which took us to around 36 or so [actually, I was so tired, I miscounted, and we had more like 42.] On Lake Ponchartraine we saw a Common Loon, a couple of Horned Grebes, several Lesser Scaup and two Brown Pelicans. A small flock of Purple Martins flew over as we returned to our car.

Sign of the day had to be the billboard advertising "Cretin Homes" – which we suppose must be a housing development, although in our hearts we wanted it to be a trailer park.

We got up an hour later than usual the next morning because it was very foggy and we are very tired. We ate a huge breakfast at the IHOP next to our hotel to start with. Then we drove to Big Branch Marsh NWR where we looked in vain for Red-cockaded Woodpeckers, but we got some other good stuff, including Mottled Ducks. We also watched a female Pine Warbler building her nest. That was a treat.

We returned to Fontainebleau State Park, where we hit the jackpot: White Pelicans, a Sora, and a glorious male Pileated Woodpecker were the highlights, and we went well over our 50-bird goal. Sue was in bed with a migraine, so J.T. and I had an early dinner at a steak and seafood place just up the road. It was awful. As soon as the hotel restaurant opened at 5:30 I got some soup and crackers for Sue. While waiting, I attempted to put together our Louisiana list. We have now completed our three-state sweep as planned.

Drove down to Bayou Sauvage NWR the following morning and visited several parts of the refuge. We saw ten or eleven new species for Louisiana. Highlights were Tricolored Herons and an Anhinga.

We took a break to have lunch in the French Quarter of New Orleans and walk around for an hour or so. Bought a few souvenirs and gifts. After lunch we took a swamp boat tour at Bayou Sauvage. It was relaxing and entertaining. Our guide, Captain Russell, was a Cajun through and through. He told us Cajun names for birds and used phrases like "I gare-own-tee" – much like Justin Wilson, the Cajun chef on PBS. We saw one adult Nutria, as well as a couple of Wild Pigs, a few Deer and numerous birds. Captain Russell had four baby Nutria(s?) in a cooler and I held one for a few minutes. Cute little guy, but still an invasive species. I suspect Captain Russell was going to drown them later.

Oh, and we saw a Raccoon in a tree. His fur was reddish, which the Captain said came from the high iron content in the local soil. We saw a squirrel with a very red tail this morning and I'll need to look in my mammal book when we get home to see whether it is a species or another local color variation.

We had a very nice dinner at Copeland's New Orleans Restaurant in Covington. The next day we planned to head back to Pensacola to fly home Saturday morning.

We left Covington a little before 8 after our third breakfast feast at IHOP. We stopped at the Mississippi Sandhill Crane NWR and got J.T. his last Mississippi birds. He had seen a Turkey Vulture on the way, and we found him a Purple Martin and a Tufted Titmouse to fill out his fifty. Once that was done we made a brief excursion to Gautier to check out another state park there. They charged two bucks to get in, and since we had our fifty birds we headed back toward Florida. On the way to Gautier we saw a church with a sign that read:

### "Wal-Mart isn't the only saving place"

...and that made the detour worth it.

Drove on to Pensacola where we registered at a Best Western near the airport. It turned out to be more like a Worst Western. It was dirty and crawling with pubescent Baptists who made 'way too much noise.

We did have time to do some more birding at Gulf Islands. This time we explored a bit of the Naval Live Oaks. We saw mostly birds we saw the previous Saturday, but Sue and I got a nice look at a Blue-headed Vireo on the nature trail near the visitor's center (not the trail we took the previous week.) The woods were dominated by live oak trees that were used in John Quincy Adams' day to build ships. There were plaques along the trail next to trees with illustrations of how the trees were "trained" to grow into useful shapes for very specific ship parts – floor, etc. Our favorite ship part had to be the "futtocks" – which inspired numerous bad puns and smart-ass comments from me. [Futtock, n. One of the curved timbers that forms a rib in the frame of a ship. [Middle English fottek, perhaps an alteration of fothok, fot, *foot*, + hok, *hook*.]

We saw a Gecko on the observation deck. [That's what a fellow from North Carolina said it was. I decided it was a Green Anole after consulting my field guide.]

On our way back to the hotel we had a light supper at a steak and ale place down the road. We re-packed our birding bags so we were nearly ready to catch our plane home in the morning. We had a great trip, knocking off our three-state birding goal, but we were exhausted.

# Chapter 11
## West Virginia, Round Two
### Wednesday, August 20 – Friday, August 22, 2003

It was on a Wednesday morning that Sue and I started driving to West Virginia area to finish up our fifty birds in that state. You may recall that we already had thirty species from the time we drove out to see Harper's Ferry a couple of years earlier. Even though it was rather the "wrong" time of year we figured how hard could it be to find twenty more species? Especially since we had chosen to do our serious birding at the Cranesville Swamp, a place with a reputation as a superb birding hotspot.

The Cranesville Swamp was one of those scattered (and very localized) areas in North America that preserved small reminders of the last Ice Age. Because of elevation and isolation, these spots often host plants long extinct in surrounding districts. This particular example of about 1600 acres is owned fittingly by the Nature Conservancy, and is open to the public. The quirkiness of the landscape also reportedly made it attractive to wildlife in general and birds in particular. It looked like the perfect place to get our last twenty species. The Conservancy warned visitors that there are "boggy areas" and they should wear appropriate footwear. It was dry when we visited. Maybe that should have been our first clue.

There was a distinct possibility that West Virginia did not like us. To begin with, we had some difficulty finding the Cranesville Swamp until we stopped and got directions and a map at a local tourist bureau. We had already made at least two complete loops around the area where the swamp was rumored to be before we realized we were not getting anywhere. We were beginning to think it was a mythical place. A sort of Appalachian Atlantis.

We made one more large (and somewhat more purposeful, now that we had a local map) loop late in the day down through the area south of Terra Alta to Route 50 and back around to Oakland, MD. When we finally located the swamp late in the afternoon, we only managed to find six species of birds and four of them were already on our list. Of course, by then it was the wrong time of day as well as the wrong time of year. At least the Wild Turkeys were new for the state list. Oh, and the Eastern Towhee. That would make us eighteen species short of our goal for the trip. We were starting to get discouraged.

There was not much out there besides the dearth, the lack, the paucity of birds. We found one seedy-looking motel near a small town in WV whose name we forgot almost immediately, but we ended up going all the way back to Oakland, Maryland and staying at the Boardroom Motel and Josie's Restaurant along Rte. 219. That would be on the extreme western border of Maryland. We had dinner at Josie's. We did not eat there twice.

Oakland itself seemed more like an extended strip mall than an actual town. Not that there weren't homes and municipal buildings and all that. It was just the feeling that everything along Rte. 219 was dominated by businesses you might see anywhere else in America. At least our motel wasn't part of one of the national chains.

Next day we headed south to Blackwater Falls State Park and the Canaan Valley area. We got a few nice birds at Blackwater, and a bunch of butterflies at Canaan Valley (pronounce locally "kuh-NANE"). My favorite was the Diana Fritillary.

Sue was seemingly ready to come home by noon, but I wanted to at least check out the Cranesville Swamp one more time, since that was our original destination to look for birds. We went back there and failed to find a single new bird, so we decided to concede that West Virginia was not willing to surrender its fiftieth species on this trip. Final total for the state

78

when we finally gave up was 41. We figured we could stop by and get our last nine or so when we headed out to get our Kentucky and Tennessee birds another day. After one final check of the swamp [and still no new birds] we headed for home.

## Chapter 12
## Arizona revisited
## Friday, March 5 – Saturday, March 13, 2004

A pleasant, but flat-toned female voice droned her message endlessly,

"CAUTION. THE MOVING WALKWAY IS ENDING"

"CAUTION. THE MOVING WALKWAY IS ENDING."

"CAUTION. THE MOVING WALKWAY IS ENDING"

It was 8:45 in the morning in Midway Airport in Chicago. It might have been an obscure corner of Dante's *Inferno*, where the souls of disgraced public address announcers went when they died. Eventually we were able to move back toward normal reality and board our plane for Phoenix.

Landing in Phoenix about 12:40 PM, we picked up our rental car and got directions to our motel. Drove up and down Van Buren Street or Road or Avenue or whatever-the-hell it was looking for the *Rodeway* Inn. We had pre-paid for eight nights as part of our Expedia package deal. We finally stopped at Gateway Community College where an extremely helpful young man told Sue, "It had to be along there nearby someplace." Um, thanks.

We checked the address again and found a *Travel* Inn at the number we had for the *Rodeway*. Turned out they had changed their name recently. Very recently. The day before, to be precise. This is a true story. Even the names have not been changed to protect the innocent. Other than the name of the motel, of course.

Anyway, our room wasn't ready so we drove over to *Bill Johnson's Big Apple* for a 2:00 o'clock lunch. The restaurant tried to be "Old West" – sawdust on the floor, waitresses wearing fake six-shooters in holsters. One waitress had ENORMOUS hair and looked like she had been there since the place opened in 1956. She also looked like she would fit right in in parts of southern New Jersey. The food was pretty good, though.

Perked up considerably, we headed out to the Desert Botanical Gardens. There were wonderful cacti on display, along with the usual Palo Verde, Creosote bushes and other desert flora. Hence the name of the place, I suppose. More to our liking, the gardens were alive with birds, most of whom were not available back home.

Life bird of the day was an Anna's Hummingbird. Like all hummers, this bird was tiny. I'm talking the size of my thumb, and I have small hands for a man. An average adult Anna's weighs about 0.15 ounces, so you could mail about six of them to your friends for the price of a first-class stamp and still have weight allowance for the envelope. That is a small bird. The male more than makes up for his diminutive size with stunning coloration. Green back, grayish breast, bright red head and throat feathers. We hip birder types refer to that red patch on the throat as his "gorget."

There were a lot of them around, and at one point we got to witness a courtship display. A female was sitting stock still in a modest Palo Verde tree. The male flew forty or fifty feet up and made a looping dive that carried him to within about six inches of the female. As he swooped by her he let out a loud un-hummingbird-like chirp. After several of these passes, he landed in a neighboring tree and flared out his crimson gorget and head feathers. Wow. There is some disagreement about how this fellow makes the loud chirp. It could be a vocalization, but it seems more likely that it is caused by flaring his tail and flight feathers at the bottom of the dive and suddenly braking. The only humans who experience that sort of deceleration are jet fighter pilots. Wow, again.

There were also numerous courting Cactus Wrens and a whole slew of Gambel's Quail – including one displaying male. We wandered around for a couple of hours trading stories with other birding types that we encountered.

Saturday morning we had a hearty breakfast at IHOP over near the Heard Museum. Then we did some birding at Encanto Park in the same general neighborhood. There were mostly the usual urban denizens about, but we did manage to find a couple of Inca Doves.

Next we went to the big Native Arts Festival at the Heard Museum. There were hundreds of exhibitors and overwhelming numbers of beautiful sculptures, carvings, paintings, etc. Sue bought a bronze eagle that was really stunning. We talked to a young woman artist who went to Westtown School! That is about twelve miles from our home. Small world.

There were a number of native dance groups performing throughout the morning. We watched Cheyennes, Hopis and Navajos. I was particularly taken with a flute solo played by one of the Cheyenne performers. Looked for a CD in the gift shop, but they seem to have mostly native music "enhanced" with New Age woo-woo crap. No thanks.

We grabbed lunch at a *Schlotzky's* once the crowds became too dense to move through the museum. Then we went out for some desert birding at White Tank Regional Park. Despite the excessive number of Leather-lunged Jerks on the trail, we managed to see a few nice birds and two lizards – a Canyon Spotted Whiptail and a Little Striped Whiptail. We also got a nice look at a Yuma Antelope Squirrel.

We (well, Sue actually) drove up to Cave Creek (the town, not the canyon) for dinner at *Crazy Ed's Satisfied Frog Restaurant and Goatsucker Saloon*. The specialty drink of the house was their chili beer. I had one with dinner and it was served with a jalapeño pepper stuck in the bottle. After we ate, we bought our friend, Tim, a T-shirt with "Drink until you want me" on the front. Also a Chili Beer shirt for me with NFL on the back – No Fuckin' Lime. Oh, and we bought a six-pack of mixed beers from their microbrewery.

We started back towards Scottsdale, except the sign for Scottsdale Road was placed New Jersey style on the wrong side[7]. So we missed our turn and ended up in Tonto National Forest. Eventually we (I was driving by now) turned back and made our way to the motel.

We were up well before the sun the following morning and on our way to Saguaro National Park – the western part. Stopped at a Cracker Barrel along the way for a large breakfast. On the way to the park we spotted a couple of Western Meadowlarks. The park itself yielded some nice stuff, including our favorite two birds with long names starting with the letter p – Phainopepla and Pyrrhuloxia. Other particularly nice birds were a couple of Black-throated Sparrows and an Ash-throated Flycatcher. Got a number of Desert Orangetips – a life butterfly. Also a couple of (probably) Sonoran Whiptails. Or maybe Western Whiptails. I could look it up.

Next we drove to Tucson Electric Park for a spring training game between the Diamondbacks and the White Sox. It was very sunny and hot. We got to see Luis Gonzalez play a few innings as well as Richie Sexon, Danny Bautista, Paul Konnerko, etc. Ate ball park junk food for lunch. Left after seven innings with the score tied at seven (the D-backs eventually won it 8-7.) We got back to our motel about 5:40, so we planned to shower and get dinner someplace.

We were going to drive up to the Grand Canyon Monday morning, but we got up sort of late and neither

---

[7] We have had a couple of experiences looking for birds in New Jersey when the signs we were looking for only appeared on the opposite side of the road where we couldn't see the front.

of us felt like driving that far. Instead we drove out toward Globe on Rte. 60 and stopped at the Boyce Thompson Arboretum State Park. The arboretum featured numerous Australian trees as well as a nice variety of birds. One of the fellows working there told us there had been a Varied Thrush and a Vermillion Flycatcher there lately. He asked if we would leave him a list of birds we saw today, and we did.

We found neither Varied Thrush nor Vermillion Flycatcher. Our best bird was a Hermit Thrush, although we enjoyed finding a Black Phoebe as well as lots of Lesser Goldfinches. The only other time we had seen the Goldfinches was near San Antonio, Texas a couple of years earlier. The habitats were varied and the rock formations impressive. So was the temperature. It was, of course, a dry heat.

At Tonto National Monument the hiking trail to the cliff dwelling was mostly vertical. The ruins were pretty typical of these things, but the views were spectacular. We got to watch the courtship display of a pair of American Kestrels on our way down. The temperature was in the nineties and it was sunny again and we both got a bit sunburned.

Next we took one of those shortcuts that take 2½ hours to cover 20 miles for all the switchbacks and one-lane spots. It was called "The Apache Trail." The scenery was, of course, breathtaking. Did I mention that we saw a Clark's Grebe on one of the lakes? You never know when the Gods of Birding are going to send a surprise. We stopped in Tempe for a nice dinner at *Gordon Birsch's*. Sue phoned Rob B., a former colleague of mine at West Chester University, and we made arrangements to meet him Tuesday evening for dinner.

Tuesday was our second blistering day in a row. 90°+ heat under an intense sun. Of course it was a DRY heat. What the hell is that about? It was bloody hot, dry or wet. We hiked around the Desert Botanical

Garden for a few hours this morning after a big breakfast at Bill Johnson's Big Apple. There were not a lot of different birds about, although we saw a Hooded Oriole and a Eurasian Collared Dove. Local mammals included several Round-tailed Ground Squirrels and Desert Cottontails – *Sylvilagus audubonii*. Sue bought a carving of Gambel's Quails at the gift shop.

We drove over to the Heard Museum around 10:30 and spent a little time and a lot of money. Sue bought another sculpture and I bought her a Navajo rug for her birthday. We had lunch at the museum's restaurant. I chose the "Arizona Salad" – romaine lettuce, roasted pine nuts, tomatoes and a guacamole-like substance in little tubular deposits that looked for all the world like goose shit. It was surprisingly bland and uninteresting despite how it looked. I bought three books at the gift shop – *Apache Diaries* and books about the Navajo code talkers and petroglyphs.

The afternoon was spent sitting around the pool at our motel (I started reading *Apache Diaries*) waiting for our room to be cleaned. Around 5:30 we drove over to Rob B.'s house and went to dinner with him a *Z Teja's*. I had the "Porcupine Shrimp" mostly because I HAD to try a dish that was described as using "blackberry wasabi." The shrimp were stuffed with crabmeat and studded with "porcupine quills" made of various dried vegetables. The wasabi, by the way, pretty much dominated the blackberry flavor in the sauce, but it was very tasty.

We crawled out around 5:30 Wednesday morning to drive to the Grand Canyon. We stopped for breakfast just south of Flagstaff. We also stopped at Red Mountain Trail and hiked back into the extinct volcano as we had the previous year. What a magical place! Clear desert air redolent of pinyon would make it a pleasant walk even without the spectacular scenery. The Gods of Birding rewarded us for our efforts by showing us a courtship display between two Prairie

85

Falcons. Wonderful! We also identified at least two races of Dark-eyed Juncos – Pink-sided and Gray-headed. I also saw a butterfly of medium size, orange and brown with a squared-off wingtip. [Probably a Golden Anglewing] Oh, and don't forget a wonderful look at a Townsend's Solitaire.

Arriving at the Grand Canyon about 12:30 or so, we decided to see if we could get a room there rather than drive all the way back to Phoenix that night. When we asked at the Bright Angel Lodge, we were offered a room in Powell Lodge for $59.13 including taxes! So there we were within spitting distance of the canyon rim. We hiked a couple of miles east of the lodge along the canyon rim and saw a few nice birds – Western Bluebirds, Pygmy Nuthatches, Hairy Woodpeckers, Mountain Chickadee and a Western Scrub Jay. There was nearly one California Condor gracing the spaces over the canyon.

Sunrise at the Grand Canyon. Breakfast at El Tovar. Life was really good. In my second historical attempt to eat a Breakfast Navajo Taco, I managed to consume all except about half of the fried bread. We took dozens (at least) of pictures of the canyon. On our way to breakfast we encountered a herd of twelve mule deer lying next to the rim trail. One buck had a very impressive rack.

We drove out to Desert View near the east end of the park and wandered around there for a short while. The tower was closed while they were taking an inventory of the attached gift shop, so we decided to mosey.

"Mosey" is one of Sue's favorite verbs. It is usually what she says when we are visiting friends and she is ready to go home. "Shall we mosey?" She tells me she used to have moseying contests with her niece and nephew when they were kids. She has challenged me to moseying contests many times. I do my best imitation of a bow-legged cowboy ambling along, and she always tells me that she has won yet again. I don't know whether I am that bad a moseyer, or whether the judge has already decided I will lose before the contest even starts. Hmm.

Sue wanted to drive across the mesas and visit Hopi Land, so we did. It was a long drive across high desert. Mile after mile of scrub vegetation and not much else. We stopped at the Hopi Cultural Center at the Second Mesa. There was a small museum with artifacts and photos and information about Hopi culture. We had lunch at the restaurant there and the menu was in Hopi with English explanations. I ordered "noqkwivi" and Sue had "chili noqkwivi." "Noqkwivi" turned out to be a bland soup of lamb and hominy with a large, roasted green chili pepper served on the side. Sue's "chili" version was spicier and greasier with a lot more lamb in it than mine. I couldn't eat much because I was still digesting breakfast anyway. Remember the Navajo taco?

We drove all the way down Rte. 87 to Tempe, stopping at Tonto Natural Bridge State Park for a brief look-see. There was a short but exciting mountain road down to the "bridge." It was actually a lovely spot. There was a large flock of White-throated Swifts flying back and forth while we walked around. We heard what might have been a towhee of some kind singing, but he wouldn't show himself, and we weren't familiar enough with western bird songs to make a positive identification.

Near the town of Happy Jack, AZ we were delayed about thirty minutes by a crew of men removing trees from the roadside. The crane operator was particularly inept, trying to move logs into position on a truck and occasionally knocking them back into the road. While we were watching this impressive display of incompetence, a Coyote ambled across the road and disappeared into the forest. Notice how I didn't say "moseyed?"

North of Tempe a series of thunderstorms rumbled across the sky east and west of us. Great gray sheets of rain punctuated by chain lightning. At one point we went through a patch of sunshine and there was an impressive rainbow. We ended up at Bill Johnson's for dinner again. I had the "Famous Pig Sandwich" (barbecued pork) and Sue had roast beef (and peach pie for dessert.) We were TIRED. We must have driven over 400 miles that day alone.

Friday morning we decided to check out South Mountain Park (2332' elevation) in Phoenix – Rob B. had highly recommended it.

We had a big breakfast at a café on Baseline Road. It was one of that dying breed of American diner culture. Friendly waitresses in starched uniforms. Local characters. Good, cheap food. A man came in while we were eating who must have weighed between five and six hundred pounds. I'm pretty sure he wasn't Konishiki, the famous (and huge) sumo wrestler. He was still impressive. In a depressing way.

The park lived up to its billing. We had a wonderful desert walk with lots of birds, a couple of as-yet-unidentified squirrels, and a couple of lizards. We drove up to the "summit" and had wonderful views of Phoenix and the mountains all around. We made a brief stop at the airport to inquire about getting an earlier flight home the next day. They told us if we got there by four AM we had a good shot at the 6:15 flight. Our current reservations were to leave around 3 PM and we wouldn't have gotten home until midnight or after.

Sue wanted to do some shopping for Navajo rugs in Scottsdale, so we had lunch over there at the *Victory Sports Bar*. Right next to a <u>Tanning Salon</u> – why would you go to a tanning salon in Phoenix? Damned if I know. Anyway, we then checked out Chief Dodge's and Ortega's. Didn't buy anything. Well, nothing big. We did get some coasters and some decorative tiles. No rugs, though.

# Chapter 13
## Assault on New England
## Sunday, June 6 – Monday, June 14, 2004

Dear friends of ours got married in Bar Harbor in June of 2004, and we decided it was the perfect opportunity to try to finish up our New England birds. We had already completed Rhode Island and had a good start on Connecticut. That left Vermont, New Hampshire, Maine, Massachusetts and the rest of our Connecticut birds.

We left the house at 6:43 the morning of Sunday, June 6 and spent most of the day driving 400 miles through rain and gray skies. Yuck. On our way across Connecticut we saw a couple of Mourning Doves, which were new to our state list. Better than nothing.

On our way to Vermont that afternoon we stopped in Massachusetts at Quabben Reservoir for a couple of hours. It wasn't raining at that particular juncture, but it was by mid-afternoon, so we didn't get a lot of birds. We did see a couple of NICE birds, however (a Prairie Warbler singing on a dead branch and an Eastern Wood-Peewee come to mind.) The park seemed to be the Chipping Sparrow Capital of New England. They were all over the place.

We got to Vermont a little after 4 and checked into the EconoLodge in Brattleboro. After getting ourselves rested a bit we drove over to Fort Dummer State Park to see when they opened in the morning – it turned out they never closed, because the place was mostly used for camping. We found an Eastern Phoebe next to the ranger station. Other than that, not much.

Brattleboro was pretty tired, dusty and shabby-looking. At least the parts we saw. We did find a nice restaurant on the Connecticut River, cleverly called the Riverview Café. We had a nice dinner there and decided to walk across the bridge because it looked like there was a lot of bird activity along there. We saw a Cedar Waxwing and two male Baltimore Orioles. There was a Mallard family with five babies on the river while we were dining. We got a fifteen-bird start on our Vermont list. Plus Massachusetts was up to 20 birds at the end of the day.

After a light breakfast the next morning at the motel, we birded around the bridge over the Connecticut River again and got several nice birds – American Redstart and Ruby-throated Hummingbird, for example. Then we drove back down to Ft. Dummer State Park where we didn't get many birds. Again. Notice how I didn't say anything about how it was even "dummer?" By the time we decided to leave Brattleboro, however, we were halfway to our goal.

We headed for Rockingham to find the "Important Bird Area" called Herrick's Cove. We drove around for over an hour without finding it or anyone who had ever even heard of it, so we gave up. It must be in hiding to keep the humans from spoiling it. Or maybe there is an "Important Bird Area" protection program we don't know about.

As a result of our total failure to locate Herrick's Cove, we decided to try Wilgus State Park and Mt. Ascutney instead. Got a bunch of birds at Wilgus and nearly burned up our brakes coming down Mt. Ascutney. They were literally smoking by the time we got to the bottom! We asked a ranger what we should do. "Keep driving. They'll cool off," said he. So that's what we did.

Unbeknownst to us, we had visited the territory where Charles Bronson had been buried less than a year earlier. The perennial tough-guy had passed away in Los Angeles the previous summer following a bout of pneumonia. Seems he also suffered from Alzheimer's and had not been doing well for at least five years. *Death Wish* indeed. His final resting place is in Brownsville, at the foot of Mt. Ascutney.

One more thing about Mt. Ascutney, then I'll move on. Promise! Mt. Ascutney is a monadnock. That means it is a lone mountain basically separated from nearby ranges. Monadnock is definitely a cool word. Possibly too long to use in a game of Scrabble®, but be sure to introduce it into conversation the next time you're at a cocktail party. It will set you apart in ways I can only guess at.

The northwest corner of the state has the only National Wildlife Refuge in Vermont, Missisquoi NWR. Near Burlington I was driving and the speed limit dropped from 65 to 55 mph. I figured it was a change that most folks would ignore, so that's what I did. There was a cop waiting for such as me and he had me dead to rights. Luckily, I was leading a pack of perhaps eight or ten other sinners and he took the easy way out and nabbed one of the laggards in the back of the group. Scared hell out of me, though. Yes, I slowed down after that. There was also a curious statue of two whale flukes along the interstate near Burlington. Should have taken a picture. The crucial words there are "should have."

Missisquoi was worth the drive! Totaling over sixty-seven hundred acres, the refuge encompassed a wide variety of habitats with lots of water. It bordered Lake Champlain on the west and was near the Canadian border to the north. Named for the Missisquoi River, it contained most of that river's delta where it emptied into Lake Champlain. We walked around two sections (visiting the main section both before and after dinner) and my current count for Vermont was 51 birds. This was a good thing, because the mosquitoes and swamp flies were feasting on us and we were not particularly excited about having to return in the morning for a couple of birds to round out the list. Instead, we could start for New Hampshire first thing. I did get a life butterfly at Missisquoi – Common Ringlet.

Swanton, VT, by the way, appeared to be a collection of road intersections crisscrossing randomly and nearly devoid of restaurants. We asked a ranger at Missisquoi for a recommendation for dinner, and she suggested driving to St. Albans. She named perhaps a half dozen restaurants there which we promptly forgot the names of.

When we got to St. Albans the traffic was backed up because the Department of Transportation had decided that early evening was a perfect time to repaint crosswalks. We finally found the Bayside Pavilion which we thought sounded like a place the ranger might have mentioned. It had a nice view of Lake Champlain and acceptable food. Busy day.

After breakfast at Mickey D.'s in Swanton, we drove to Montpelier where we hit Rte. 2 and took it across to New Hampshire.

The plan was to visit Umbagog Lake NWR near the town of Errol, since it sounded like a good birding spot. We got a couple of decent birds along the road (Common Loon on the Androscoggin River comes to mind) and a Belted Kingfisher at Umbagog itself. The ranger at Umbagog was almost too busy to tell us anything useful. There was a short, swamp-fly-infested hiking trail with a blind at the lake. We found very little there. In fact, we only found six species at Umbagog. Not a propitious start for New Hampshire.

Sue vetoed my suggestion that we stay overnight in Errol and try our luck at morning birding the next day, not that I protested very strenuously. So we drove on to Maine. Had lunch at a Subway in some small town. Stopped at a little park in Skowhagen and did a little birding. There was a pair of Ospreys fishing on the river as well as a Bald Eagle. They were worth the stop. We continued on to Orono where we could find only one motel (we'd had a long day.) Ended up in Bangor where we found a Hampton Inn.

Dinner was at Bugaboo's where the food was excellent and we were entertained by talking bison and moose heads and a talking pine tree. You had to be there. Sue ran the car through a car wash before we returned to the motel. We planned to check out Sunkhaze Meadows NWR north of Old Town the next morning.

After breakfast we started looking for Sunkhaze Meadows NWR which appeared on the map to be between Milford and Casington. We drove by a sign for it in Milford, thinking the main entrance must be elsewhere. There should be a sign, surely, near the other entrance. Casington evidently existed only in the fevered minds of Rand-McNally's mapmakers. We drove well up Rte. 2 and found nothing. So we drove all the way back to Milford thinking maybe that sign marked the entrance after all. The sign turned out to mark a boat launch where we could have put our canoes in, if we had had any. Back up Rte.2 we went until we hit Greenbush.

In desperation, we stopped and got directions from a heating contractor who actually knew how to get there!. Using his instructions we found the dirt road and made it to the actual hiking trail. After walking the trail a while we decided to try along the roadway. We kept hearing a warbler sort of call – zeet zeet zeet diddle-ee – and after a good 10-15 minutes of frustration (on our part, the bird was okay with it) a male Mourning Warbler presented himself for inspection. Nice bird! Sue's fuel gauge alarm went off, so we filled up as soon as we got back to Old Town.

We stopped at the ranger station to get directions to Calder Pond. The sign on the door said "Open Monday through Friday 7:30 AM to 4 PM. It was 9:30 AM. They were, of course, closed.

We decided to head on down to Acadia National Park and Bar Harbor and spent the afternoon driving the loop road in the park. Best birds there were Black

Guillemots and Common Eiders. We walked around a bit of the nature trail at Jordan Pond and saw some Common Mergansers and a Flicker. Then we checked into our motel (which was very near the entrance to the park and rated a stage three on the motel deterioration scale.) This scale runs from Stage 1: a brand new motel. To Stage 4: Run down and dirty. Stage 3 is basically a shabby stage. It was reasonably clean, but showing a lot of wear and tear.

That evening we went into Bar Harbor and walked around a bit. Had dinner outdoors at Rupununi's. I had lobster and Sue had steak. It only came to $38 including drinks. Very reasonable!

We got up around six and drove in to Bar Harbor. Had the breakfast buffet at Bunny's Downeast Restaurant. The food was pretty good except for the powdered eggs. Then we went to the nature trail at Sieur Mont (or whatever.) It was cloudy. It was drizzly. It was cold. The birds were smarter than we were. They slept in. We decided to move on. Looked for the Peregrine Falcons reportedly nesting at Precipice. No luck. (If a centipede a quart, a velocipede a pint, how much did a precipice? Thanks Mom.)

We stopped at Sand Beach and saw 3 Black Guillemots, 10-12 Common Eiders, plus a few cormorants and gulls. Then we went back to Jordan Pond. By then the sun had finally come out. We started on the nature trail around the pond and decided to take a trail up the mountain. Finally found some really nice birds – Black-throated Green Warbler, Pileated Woodpecker, Red-breasted Nuthatch and Blackburnian Warblers. Our Maine list was up to 47 by my then-current calculation.

Drove back to Bar Harbor for a while. Sue got her hair cut. We had lunch at the Quarterdeck and then stopped and got tickets for a whale watching cruise the next day at noon. We decided to explore some more of Mt. Desert Island (pronounced "dessert" by some, "desert" by others) and spent several hours driving around the western side. Stopped at Bass Harbor Head Light and took a few pictures.

Finally made our way back to Precipice, after a brief stop at the top of Mount Cadillac for the view and more pictures. This time we met a ranger on a seasonal assignment. He was a pleasant young chap from Pittsburgh. As we were visiting I spotted two Peregrines flying in from the northeast. Bird #48 for Maine, if my count was accurate. Then we (actually Sue) decided to stop at the Bar Harbor Inn to see if our friends, Tim and Sally had arrived. We met up with them and they took us to Gaylyn's for a lovely dinner. All in all, a very busy and delightful day.

We drove by a little church called "Back Side Redemption" and I wondered whether the preacher concentrated on saving his flock's collective butts. Hmm.

We went to Bunny's again for breakfast around 6:30. Then we returned to the nature trail that was a bust the previous day because of the rain. Oh, by the way, it was 46° that morning when we started out. Brrrrrr.

The nature trail was MUCH better that day. We got nice looks at Redstarts, a Black-throated Green Warbler, another Pileated Woodpecker and a juvenile Swainson's Thrush. Plus we heard a Winter Wren. Oh, and a Least Flycatcher. We stopped at Precipice and the Peregrines were consistently not to be seen. The ranger said the young fledged last week, so activity around the nest was minimal. We did find a Chestnut-sided Warbler, however.

We went in to Bar Harbor to do a little shopping and wait for the Whale Watch boat. The boat sailed at noon. The wind was cold and the boat was fast. We took our rain jackets for windbreakers. Good idea. We stopped at Petit Manan Island and saw Puffins and

Razorbills and Guillemots and lots of terns. Then to the open sea about 20 miles out. I spotted the first whale and it turned out to be a Minke female with a calf. The boat stayed around the same area for about 45 minutes and we got a lot of good looks at mother and calf. Very cool. Also saw a couple of Gannets and a Wilson's Storm Petrel. The on-board "naturalist" misidentified a Common Loon as a juvenile Gannet. Yikes.

Back in Bah Hahbah[8] we caught some dinner at a restaurant we had not yet tried. I had fish and chips and Sue had spaghetti and the check came to $10 more than we spent last night for steak and lobster. Harumph.

We left Bah Hahbah a little after six the next morning. Breakfast at Mickey D's on the road. Got to New Hampshire about 10:30 or so. Stopped at an information booth in Portsmouth and got directions to Great Bay NWR. Walked both trails at the refuge and got our state list up to 40. Birded our way down the coast toward Massachusetts and got up to 46. NO, 47!

We started to bird in Massachusetts a bit but finally decided to go back and finish New Hampshire off. We checked into a hotel near Portsmouth and there was a Cardinal singing outside our room as we unloaded our luggage. Number 48! So we went over to the refuge (2 or 3 miles from our motel) figuring we could find 2 more birds without much trouble.

A Black Duck showed up for number 49. Nice. We were sitting on a bench in the woods by a stream saying a Belted Kingfisher would make a nice 50th bird for New Hampshire when two of them actually flew by! Then I realized we had seen one earlier up at Umbagog. Nuts. The Gods of Birding are going to make us work for that last bird...

---

[8] That is how it is pronounced by the locals.

Long day! We started out before six. Breakfast at Mickey D.'s and then over to Great Bay NWR to look for bird #50. On the way over we spotted a Northern Flicker along the road. He did the trick. We immediately headed for Massachusetts to try our luck at Parker River NWR on Plum Island.

There was a lot going on there – Bobolinks and Willets and Least Terns among others. We hit the magic 50+ mark by 9:30 and headed for our last quest state for the trip, Connecticut. We decided to return to the McKinney Saltmarsh Meadows NWR (or whatever the official name is) where we had some luck on our last trip up there. We only needed a handful of birds (14 or so) and figured it shouldn't be too hard. Of course we hadn't figured rain into our equation. We both were determined to finish up this part of the quest come hell or high water. Donning rain jackets, we slogged through forest, along marsh and across fields, ending with 54 Connecticut birds.

Hallelujah! That finished our 25th state, if my calculations were correct. They were usually off by at least a couple. We finished counting our birds by about 3:30 and decided to head for home early. We got there around 10 o'clock.

# Chapter 14
## Hawai'i, Parts One A and B
### Sunday, January 2 - Thursday, January 6
### and Monday, January 31 - Wednesday, February 2, 2005

Our first trip to Hawai'i was planned as a break in a much longer trip to New Zealand. The flight time to New Zealand was so daunting we decided to spend a few days on Oahu on the way there and see how many birds we could get. It was a great lesson in the limits of island biodiversity.

For readers who haven't heard that term, "island biodiversity" refers to the range of species that live in a given, clearly defined geographic space. It doesn't have to be an island. It can be land isolated by surrounding mountains or desert. The premise is that smaller areas can only support a limited number of species. The larger the area, the greater the possible biodiversity. After reading extensively on the subject, I was about to get an object lesson on Oahu.

We got to the Philadelphia Airport Sunday morning around 6 AM. The check-in was reasonably smooth. Breakfast fell in the range between mediocre and awful. My "Scrambled Egg Platter" consisted of:

1. Powdered eggs served right around body temperature
2. Home fries served cold (only revenge should be served this way)
3. Half-cooked bacon
4. Very dry toast the consistency of styrofoam and with a similar flavor
5. Coffee – at least it was hot

Sue had a cold Belgian waffle with whipped cream and apples with a cup of orange juice. At a little before 8 and we saw our plane already being serviced at the gate. On-time service from Northwest Airlines was not something we expected.

We landed in Detroit about 11 AM. The only smoking area was at the Fox Skybox Bar. So we had glasses of water and fruit plates so Sue could smoke a couple of cigarettes. We got to our Honolulu connecting flight in time for general boarding, so we walked right on. The weather outside was rainy, and one of the flight attendants told someone we would probably leave fifteen minutes or so late to help folks make connections. That was around noon.

At 1:10 PM we were still sitting on the ground in Detroit. We almost started out at about 1:05, but had to return to the gate for two more "unaccompanied minors." Company policy prohibited leaving without such waifs. Probably the humane thing to do, but we were more than an hour behind. They started showing the safety video. Again. I had a pretty good idea by now about where the personal flotation devices were and how to wear one. I was pretty confident that I knew how to get my oxygen mask on "should it become necessary." My personal opinion is that in a major emergency I may as well pray to the Gods of Birding for a giant Eagle to swoop down and save my ass.

By 1:45 we were airborne at last. The woman seated behind me talked non-stop from the time she boarded. She may have mastered the art of circular breathing, because she never seemed to pause. I hoped she would rest her mouth soon after we became airborne. Otherwise we might have had a Honolulu Homicide. I planned as my defense to claim insanity brought on by Prattle Fatigue, a medical condition I had just discovered.

We landed in Hawai'i around 10 PM local time. The good news was that our flight from Detroit to Honolulu was fairly smooth, although we left Detroit about an hour and a half behind schedule. We had stunning views of Mt. St. Helens and Mt. Rainier as we flew past Washington. The STATE not the city!

The bad news was that our luggage went to Minneapolis and arrived on a flight that got here over an hour after ours. This won us a chance to stand around the baggage carousel TWICE. In between we got to wait in line to file a missing luggage report. By the time we got through the red tape, our suitcases were already taking their second or third lap around the carousel. Wonder if Northwest planned all of that as a sort of practical joke.

We picked up our rental car and found The Breakers Hotel on Beachwalk without much trouble. It was a charming relic of the 1950s, we guessed. Biding its time with quiet dignity until some developer realized that a high rise hotel on the spot would make him about a bazillion dollars.

We checked in and then dealt with getting a temporary parking card. This involved red tape on a purely local and private level. Found the parking lot a couple of blocks away and walked back to the hotel. It was a little past 3 AM back home, so we had been up for nearly 24 hours. Tired but totally exhausted.

Up before 6 Monday morning, we had breakfast in the next block at the Islander Coffee House on Lewers Street. Wandered around the area near our hotel and saw some good birds. There were quite a few garden-variety Rock Pigeons flying around, but the cool thing was that they were all pure white, like the ones pulled out of magician's hats or released at tacky weddings. A few Pacific Golden-Plovers walked about the lawns looking for invertebrates for breakfast. They looked astonishingly similar to American Golden-Plovers that we occasionally saw closer to home, although our field guide assured us they are different species. My personal favorite for this walk was the Red Junglefowl. You non-birders probably know them by the more prosaic name of Wild Chickens.

Next we walked over to Kapiolani Park which was rumored to have good populations of some birds we really wanted to find. We found exactly none of the promised species, but it was a very pretty walk. On our way back to the hotel we checked out a number of souvenir shops looking to add to my kitsch collection. There were a couple of strong candidates among a wonderful variety of tacky tiki (say that fast three times) carvings. We had lunch at a Japanese noodle shop. I enjoyed it much more than Sue did, I fear.[9]

We were picked up for our pre-arranged Oahu Nature Tour around 1:35 PM. Sue's camera died before we started. Aargh. The group included David, our guide, plus couples from Wales, Texas, and Kansas, a woman from Virginia and two Canadian girls who were on vacation from teaching ESL in Japan.

David was a thin wisp of a man about 55-60 years old. He knew a ton of information about local history and botany, much less about birds. He talked nearly non-stop for the entire trip, which was NOT really necessary. His political correctness made his description of a visit to the famous leper colony on Molokai convoluted and borderline amusing, at least to an old cynic like me. Referring to the lepers as "sufferers from Hansen's Disease" seemed a bit too much.

A number of the other participants were birders, and we all helped one another with finding and identifying birds. There were three or four copies of *Hawaii's Birds* along plus a nice chart and a *Birders' Guide to Hawai'i*. Sue and I never would have spotted the White-rumped Shama if one of the others hadn't pointed it out.

Our first stop on the tour was at the Paiko Lagoon Wildlife Sanctuary where we got nice looks at our first endemic – the Hawaiian Coot. It looks astonishingly like the American Coot and the Eurasian Coot, so maybe we would need to do a DNA analysis to notice the difference. In any case, a lifer is a lifer. We also saw a Hawaiian Black-necked Stilt which is

---

[9] I lived in Japan from 1990-1992 and loved the food. This was a few years before I met Sue.

classified as a subspecies and looks just like other Black-necked Stilts we have seen in places like Delaware. Still...Near one of the observation points we saw a *coconut* that had sprouted. THAT we don't see back home.

Next stop was at Hanauma Bay which produced no new birds. No, wait, that was where we saw both Brown and Red-footed Boobies soaring offshore. More life birds. Ho-hum. At Halona Cove there were a number of Green Sea Turtles feeding close to the shore along with a handful of snorkelers who were following them. This was where some of the famous beach scenes in *From Here to Eternity* were filmed. I was more interested in the blowhole that was shooting impressive sprays of seawater every couple of minutes. Tried to take a picture of a spray, but got a lot of shots of water gushing back into the hole. Bad timing. My forte.

At the Ulupou Heiau, David was in his glory. Heiau is Polynesian for a sort of temple. He knew tons about traditional Hawaiian culture as well as a lot about the native plant life. For us, the highlight of the Heiau was a great look at a White-rumped Shama. NOT a native bird, but a pretty one and it counts! So there.

The last stop on this tour was at the famous Pali Lookout. Mark Twain allegedly thought the view from there was one of the most beautiful on our planet. We would not disagree with that assessment. From the aquamarine of Kaneohe Bay to the dramatic dark cliffs of the Koolau volcano, it is breathtaking.

We saw some wonderful birds, but the Great Frigatebird would have to get the prize for the most spectacular and generous. I took some close-up shots of a Red-vented Bulbul and hoped they came out. During the day we identified 24 species. I was starting to think 50 species might be tough on Oahu. Dinner, at the recommendation of a fellow at The Breakers, was at a smorgasbord place not far from our hotel. It was grubby, yet depressing. We didn't ask that fellow for a second recommendation.

We got up early Tuesday and Sue drove us to Pearl Harbor for our planned visit to the Arizona Memorial. We got there when they opened, so there were only a couple of hundred people in line ahead of us! Seriously. They opened at 7:30 and our tickets to actually go out to the memorial were for the 8:45 presentation. They showed us a movie about the Japanese attack and then took us by boat out to the ship. It was well done and well-run and very moving.

Our next stop was the Wahiawa Botanical Gardens in, um, er, ah, Wahiawa. The trees and plants were impressive, but the expected birds were not. Stuff we saw yesterday. Yawn. Japanese White-eyes and Red-vented Bulbuls mostly. We did see a male Red Jungle Fowl and later a hen and 3-4 chicks. For those of you who were not paying attention yesterday, Red Jungle Fowl are the ancestors of all modern breeds of domestic chickens. The population in Hawai'i descends from birds introduced from Southeast Asia, so YES we can count them. It's our list, dammit. We had driven past the Botanical Gardens on our way out, since it was cleverly marked by nearly one sign. We finally asked a couple of young men where it was, and they agreed to tell us in exchange for a couple of cigarettes.

We continued north (Sue did all the driving today) on the Interstate – think about that for a minute – and had lunch at Hale'iwa on the North Shore. The restaurant was called – are you ready for this – The Breakers. Clever, eh? We continued along and found an Audubon Nature Center at Waimea Valley. Probably THE Audubon Nature Center at Waimea Valley, I suppose. We walked around there for an hour or so. Saw lots of Common Waxbills, Red-vented Bulbuls, Zebra and Spotted doves and Hawaiian Moorhens. Oh, and 4-5 mongooses. Mongeese? Whatever. We also finally saw some Red-whiskered Bulbuls, so we were exactly half way to our 50-bird goal.

We drove back to Waikiki and Sue took her camera to the shop next to the Islander Coffee House. Her shutter was stuck, so she decided to just buy a new camera. We had a nice dinner at Arancino, the Italian place across from our hotel. I had seafood spaghetti and Sue had fettuccine with asparagus and prosciutto. We only walked about two and one-quarter miles that day.

News Item: However many days it was after the full moon meant it was time for the annual jellyfish invasion. They would be there until Friday or so. Of course, by then we would be on our way to New Zealand, but that is another story.

Still hanging out in Waikiki. We got going about 5:30 that morning. Breakfast at the Island Coffee House again. Oahu Nature Tours picked us up at seven for our "rainforest hike." We hiked parts of the Mano Cliff Trail and the Puu Ohia Trail.

Our guide, Matt, showed us numerous endemic plants as well as a very tiny endemic snail. There was not much in the way of birds other than the fleeting glimpse I got of a pair of Apapanes. They were high in the canopy, and when I described them as "small red birds" our guide assured me that they had to be Apapanes. Other than that, nothing new.

We took numerous pictures of spectacular scenery. At the top of Mount Tantalus, we were at the highest point on Oahu. The elevation at the top was around 2000-2100 feet plus according to my GPS receiver. We stopped at a lookout in Pu'u Wala Kaa State Park on the way back. The name means something like "Hill that the sweet potatoes roll down." Pu'u= hill; Wala= sweet potato; Kaa= roll. We walked about four miles that day.

We slept in the next morning. Well, we didn't get to breakfast at the Islander Coffee House until 6:30. I had Spam and eggs today. Yum. Spam was very popular in Hawai'i. Our trip of the day was a hike to a waterfall. The hike was only about two miles or so, but the trail was steep and muddy in places. There was a rude group at the waterfall itself led by a fellow with a NY City accent. That figures. The group was splashing about in the pools and making more noise than a quail's ass in chokecherry season, as my Dad would have said. Sue spotted a Red-billed Leiothrix along the trail, and we both got good looks at it. We stopped at Pali Lookout again on the way back (elevation 1170'). The weather started out rainy and misty, but it cleared beautifully by mid-morning. We spotted a White-tailed Tropicbird at Pali, too, so it was a productive trip. David was our leader again. The other hikers included two couples from Ohio and Denver, two women from Tokyo (Japanese this time), and a woman from Wellington, NZ! She gave us the address and phone number of folks to contact in Wellington, should we find ourselves at loose ends there.

After our return to Waikiki, we had lunch at Kelley O'Neil's Pub. Sue dropped off a couple of prescriptions at a pharmacy and we went shopping while waiting for the pills. We found a wonderfully tacky tiki for my kitsch collection. We also located a phantom Border's Bookstore after some wandering. I picked up a Hawaiian language CD and several books to read on the plane to New Zealand. Speaking of the plane to New Zealand, it was time to pack and get ready to boogie.

Friday, January 7, 2005. Gotcha! There was no Friday that week. We crossed the International Date Line in the middle of the night and skipped Friday.

Monday (sort of) January 31 (sort of)

105

This was going to be a week with two Mondays to balance the week with no Friday. Got up about 3:45 that morning and rode the 4:30 shuttle to the Auckland Airport. Checked in. Paid our departure fees ($25 NZ each) and cleared security in plenty of time for our 7 o'clock departure for Sydney. Had a smooth flight to the West Island, as the Kiwis call Australia. Our connection in Sydney was very tight and there was confusion over which gate we were to report to. Our flight number had changed, and as we were going to one gate as we had been told to, we were being paged to return to the one where we were told the wrong one. Did you follow that? I'll try again. The flight number we ended up taking did not match our tickets. We were sent FROM Gate 51 to Gate 55, but were paged to report immediately to Gate 51, as our flight was about to leave. Bottom line – we made our plane, but Sue never had a chance for a smoke. The plane was not full, so folks spread out to take advantage of the empty seats. Sue had a three-seat center row to herself – she had room for a wee lie down. I started reading Michael King's *The Penguin History of New Zealand* that I bought in Auckland. Oh, we crossed the dateline, so it was technically Sunday again.] My effing light kept going off and on at random. Would turn it off next cycle... Done! Zzzzzzzzzz.

Monday, January 31, 2005. Again. 12:01 AM.

Well, we got to Honolulu in one piece. Our luggage seemed to have stayed in Sydney, however. Air Canada promised that it should be there the next day. We'd see. The Honolulu Airport Hotel was pretty shabby, I noticed. The room was clean, though. As soon as we checked in (around 11:45 PM) we walked to the Chevron mini-mart a loooooooong block away so Sue could get cigarettes. Oh, before I forget, the plane we came in on was not more than half full, yet they had *inadequate food* – so there were no choices of entrée. The second meal consisted of "lasagna" that reminded us more of some sort of glue. There was a suggestion

in mine that someone had thought about tomato sauce at some time in their lives. We were not impressed with Air Canada. Did I mention that the flight TIME was changed as well as the number? We'd laugh some day...

We had breakfast in the morning there at the hotel. Then we took a city bus in to Honolulu and did some shopping. We bought toothbrushes, toothpaste, disposable razors and deodorant, in case our bags didn't show up. Oh, and T-shirts. I got some Kona coffee for a friend. We bought a lei for Syd [our granddaughter]. Came back to the hotel and napped most of the afternoon. Air Canada called about 1:30 PM to say our bags were definitely coming. There were flood watches for Kauai that night. I hoped our flight wasn't delayed the next day. We were ready to go home! Our bags showed up a little after midnight.

2:00 PM Honolulu Airport.
Breakfast at the hotel. Sue did two loads of wash that morning. We left the hotel about 11:15 on the shuttle. Hurry up and wait. Hard to say what was getting more annoying there at the airport. Security and no-smoking announcements or whiny Hawaiian music. SPARE US!

10:00 PM PST, San Francisco.
We got there without problems other than fatigue. The Captain or Head Stewardess (oops, Flight Attendant) or somebody said we would be continuing on to Minneapolis on the same plane, so at least we didn't have to run around looking for our next gate. The Bay Area looked incredibly beautiful in the clear air going in – reminded me of gold lame on black velvet for some reason. I was almost surprised that the lights didn't morph into a portrait of Elvis. We were a lot closer to home than we had been a couple of days before...

Wednesday, February 2, 2005.

Our connection in Minneapolis was tight – we walked briskly from terminal C to terminal G and got there about a half hour before our flight was to leave. No way our checked luggage got transferred that quickly. Our departure was delayed slightly and the plane had to be de-iced before takeoff. Other than that, everything went smoothly. We got to Philly about 11:30 AM. Ben met us at baggage claim and, wonder of wonders, so did our luggage!

So we ended the trip with 30 birds on Oahu. Something over 90 bird species have been reported and accepted by some committee as "countable" for Oahu. That means we were able to locate in just a couple of days roughly one-third of the possible species to be found there. Considering the fact that other states where we had very limited time to look we found only 12-14% of the listable birds, we did very well indeed on Oahu. Of course we still needed twenty more birds and would just have to go back to Hawai'i for a second time.

# Chapter 15
## Rocky Mountain States – Colorado, Idaho, Utah and Wyoming
### Wednesday, April 27 – Saturday, May 7, 2005

Some days seem to last much longer than twenty-four hours. This trip began with one of those. Rising around 5:20 AM, we had a quick breakfast at home. Then we drove to my son's house so he could drive us to the Philadelphia Airport. We got through security a couple of hours before our scheduled departure. I killed time by reading the most recent issue of *Audubon*, walking around, and reading the magazine rack. Yawn.

We boarded our plane more or less on time, but had to wait while some mechanical problem was addressed. By the time we took off we were more than an hour late. Of course, that meant we missed our connection in St. Louis. We actually got there in time, but they had already closed the gate and shifted us to a later flight. The later flight left about an hour and a half later than later.

During the flight to Denver we got to fill out a customer satisfaction survey. Cynical old me figured it was a psychological ploy to defuse our anger. Mine was closer to fury. I still let them know that I thought they were a bunch of incompetent nitwits. Not that I thought they really cared, nor would anyone actually read the surveys. The ploy worked, though. My anger was pretty much dissipated by the time I finished the form. I think they call the field that dreams up such things "industrial psychology." I actually met an industrial psychologist once and took an immediate dislike to him.

By the time we got to Denver, picked up our car and got to our hotel it was 6:40 PM or so. We had tickets for the Rockies game that started at 6:30. I called the ticket office and they offered us tickets for tomorrow afternoon. We were so far beyond tired that I was ready to lose the money for the tickets. Anyway, we walked over to a local Applebee's and had a nice dinner. Whatever it was. Then to bed for some much-needed rest.

The following today began with breakfast at the Sleep Inn – lots of choices and good food. Breakfast at American motels is always a crap shoot. This time we won.

Since we had tickets for the 1:05 Rockies game, we decided to check out a couple of National Wildlife Refuges around Denver in the morning. We made our way to Rocky Mountain Arsenal NWR only to find that it is only open to the public on weekends. It was Thursday.

Next we drove over to Two Ponds NWR on the west side of town. A sign at the entrance explained that it would open on May 1. It was April 28. Despite the good breakfast, the day was starting to turn sour.

Looking for an alternate way to kill time before the ballgame, we drove to the cleverly-named City Park in Denver where we thought maybe we could visit the Science Museum, if nothing else was happening. It turned out it was hopping with birds! The PARK, not the museum. There were literally hundreds of Double-crested Cormorants and Black-crowned Night-herons nesting in the trees. Well, dozens anyway. Definitely more than two. Plus a few Western Grebes and at least one Clark's Grebe on the lake. We got 27 or 28 species just in the park. We never did actually get around to checking out the Science Museum.

Satisfied with our propitious start on getting fifty birds in Colorado, we went to Coor's Field for some baseball. Did I mention that last night's game ended up snowed out? And they gave us tickets to a double header this afternoon? I thought not. It had been hovering around the freezing point all day – raining and snowing off and on. We got to the ballpark early and had our mandatory hot dogs. Chatted with some nice

110

folks who sell refreshments as a means of raising money for their church. They were not very busy for some reason.

While we wandered around waiting for batting practice to start, a short, stout gentleman with white hair and an impressive moustache told us that both games had been postponed. Until August. We went to the service window and applied for a refund. They even refunded our parking fee on the way out. Of course, Ticketmaster still kept their commission, even though we ended up with no tickets. Does that seem right?

After sorting all of that out, we drove up to Evan, Colorado and got a room at another Sleep Inn. Made a quick run out to Greeley and got information about, and a map of the Pawnee National Grassland. We did some birding at the Grassland and saw lots of Kestrels, a few White-crowned Sparrows and two Blue-gray Gnatcatchers. Hey, they were new to our Colorado list.

Dinner that evening was at the *Western Sizzler Steakhouse* in Evan. We were not impressed. It was still snowing. The weather service folks were calling for one to three inches that night. We were beginning to suspect that coming to the Rockies at the end of April might not have been the best idea we had ever had.

It was snowing and cold Friday morning when we started out. We decided to try to find a White Pelican nesting colony rumored to be about 20 miles east of Greeley on route 34. Plenty of white snow, no pelicans at all. White or otherwise. Our Colorado count was stuck at 39, but we still had to return to Denver to fly home.

The sun seemed to be trying its best to come through, so we decided to go ahead and drive to Wyoming as planned. The weather had been so stinko we were beginning to wonder whether this whole trip might be a bust.

We managed to find Hutton Lake NWR south of Laramie despite awful directions and an unpaved, snow-covered road. Sue let me drive that bit, since people like me who grew in the snow belt of Central New York generally consider anything under two or three feet of snow just a minor inconvenience. We couldn't actually get to the lake, but along the way we saw lots of prairie dogs and pronghorns as well as Chestnut-collared Longspurs which was a lifer for both of us.

We took I-80 all the way to Rock Springs (over 200 miles.) We half-heartedly washed the car to get the worst of the caked-on dirt off. Dinner was barbecued beef sandwiches at *Pam's Barbecue*. The place was described in *Hidden Wyoming* as "no frills." They got that right. The "restaurant" was basically a large, undecorated room with some tables in it. The waitress was friendly and certainly not very busy! The sandwiches were delicious as promised, and Sue got a take-out slice of sweet potato pie.

It was snowing lightly when we got up Saturday. We had breakfast in the restaurant downstairs at the Sleep Inn. It was filling. Not bad. Not special. Anyway we were on the road before 7. Drove to Seedskadee NWR through fog and blowing snow. Not a propitious beginning, but by the time we got to the refuge around 8 the clouds were breaking up.

The Gods of Birding were smiling on us. We saw a Franklin's Gull along the way which I thought was a lifer for both of us. That turned out to be wrong. Not that it was a Franklin's Gull, it simply turned out we had already seen one in New Jersey back in '97. There was also a Golden Eagle hunting near the road at one point. Not a lifer, but a wonderful bird any time you see one. Definitely new for the Wyoming list.

At Seedskadie we saw tons of great birds – Mountain Bluebirds, Sandhill Cranes, Sage Sparrows and Thrashers, a dozen White Pelicans, 2 Trumpeter Swans (definitely life bird for both of us) and SO MUCH MORE! For just $19.95... Sorry, I thought I was doing an infomercial there for a second. We did see a couple of herds of Pronghorns and good numbers of ground squirrels in addition to the birds. Oh, our species total – just for Seedskadie – was 42.

We next drove up to the town of Lander and checked in at the Pronghorn Lodge. There was a huge statue of an Elk out front for some reason. Wouldn't you think they would have a statue of a pronghorn? Don't know where I get these crazy ideas.

Lunch was at the Gannet Grill about a block from here. Not that there were any Gannets in Colorado as far as we knew, but we tended to choose restaurants with birds' names in them when available. Later research confirmed that there were no records of a Gannet ever being seen in Wyoming. Um, it is too far from the ocean for one thing.

We went over to Sinks Canyon State Park for a hike of some substance (steep and snowy) and saw lots of Townsend's Solitaires and four Clark's Nutcrackers (a lifer for Sue.) At the end of the day our Wyoming total was up to 58 species. Crossed another state off the list.

Sue dropped me off in beautiful downtown Lander, and I visited two bookstores. At the first one I found a used (but great condition) copy of *Where the Birds Are* for six bucks. Since our old copy was disintegrating, I bought it. Then I crossed the street to another bookstore where I bought two books of essays and poems by Wyoming writers.

Breakfast was at the Oxbow Grill Sunday morning in Lander – "Pleasin' people with good cookin'." Worked for us. Drove across beautiful goddam scenery all morning.[10] Got to Teton National Park around 11 or so.

---

[10] This is an oblique reference to Sue's "Uncle" Earl who had not travelled much. When he returned from a trip out west, he said they saw nothing but goddam beautiful scenery.

Birded a trail near the entrance to the park. Lots of good looks at good birds including a Red-naped Sapsucker and a juvenile Golden Eagle. Made our way to Jackson and had a late lunch at the Merry Piglets Mexican Grill. Found our motel in Teton Village and took a break. It was between the ski season and summer, so the "village" was nearly deserted.

Then we drove over to Elk National Refuge, where (of course!) we saw eleven Bighorn Sheep. Go figure. We did see a herd of Elk down the road from Teton Village...

We had breakfast in our room Monday – stuff we got Sunday at the Albertson's in Jackson. Because of the off season, many restaurants and shops were closed. We went looking for birds in Grand Teton National Park again. The trails still had a lot of snow (several feet deep in many places) and we were pretty tired from the previous day, so our success was limited at best. We drove up as close to Yellowstone as the road allowed and did see a pair of Barrow's Goldeneyes, a couple of Sandhill Cranes, some Common Redpolls, a Belted Kingfisher and some Bison. We went back to our hotel and took it easy the rest of the day. At that point our Wyoming total had reached 75 species. It was time to move on!

The following day we drove close to 450 miles. Started by driving to Gray's Lake NWR in Idaho. The refuge was touted as the largest hardstem bulrush marsh in North America. We still have no idea of the significance of that claim. There is actually no "lake" per se, only an extensive marsh. We stayed there an hour or so checking out some of the wet meadows and grasslands.

At one of our stops near the road, there were several Sandhill Cranes doing their courtship dance. Imagine five-foot-tall mostly gray and brown birds hopping about with wings spread and heads bobbing. A ballet with only the trills of the cranes for musical accompaniment. Goosebump time. Again. By the time we left Gray's lake, our Idaho list was already at 45 species!

We continued south to Bear Lake NWR where we picked up another 15 species or so for a total of around 60 for the state. Well, actually it was only 14 species, so our total was actually 59. It was over fifty, in any case and time to move on. Idaho turned out to be our quickest 50 birds of all the states. We were there less than three hours.

Back to Wyoming for a brief visit to Fossil Butte National Monument and a short hike on one of the trails there. The place contained a wide variety of some of the best-preserved fossils in North America. The weather was cold and windy. It made us nostalgic for the lost sub-tropical climate. We should have gone about seventy million years earlier.

On our way back from Fossil Butte we saw two Bald Eagles at different spots. The second one was eating something furry on the top crossbar to a ranch entrance gate. There was a Magpie sitting next to him, evidently hoping for some leftovers. Other highlights for the day included Long-billed Curlews (lifer, lifer!) a couple more Trumpeter Swans, Clark's and Western Grebes, hundreds of Pronghorns and a Golden Eagle next to the road feeding on a deer carcass. Phew.

We had a nice dinner at the Sidewinder Grill in Jackson that night. The next morning we planned to head for the Flaming Gorge and our assault on the birds of Utah.

We were up well before six the following morning and on the road a little after 6:30. Stopped in Jackson and filled up our gas tank. We went down Route 191 through Rock Springs to the Flaming Gorge. Stopped briefly at the Firehole in the gorge. A maintenance fellow working at the visitor center gave us a map of the gorge.

We stopped in Dutch John for a bite of lunch at a diner/souvenir shop/mostly fly-fishing gear place. On our way to Vernal we spotted a few birds, including a Clark's Nutcracker. In Vernal we checked into a Best Western (we chose "Antlers" over "Dinosaur" because the latter was being invaded by a busload of schoolchildren.) After we schlepped our stuff to our room we drove out to Ouray NWR. Stopped briefly at Pelican Lake and got a bunch of waterfowl (duh.) At Ouray we drove the five-mile auto route. We got lots of birds, but the biggest kick was seeing three porcupines up in trees!

Back in Vernal we got some snack food at the local Wal-Mart. When we returned to the motel we spent fifteen minutes relaxing in the Jacuzzi. Current Utah bird count was 43. Possibly 44 if our "other bird" last time was a Loggerhead Shrike...(It wasn't. Our first two Utah birds were a Western Kingbird and a Common Raven.)

We got up early and returned to Ouray NWR the next morning. Got there around seven and it was worth the trip. We saw 4 or 5 porcupines plus more than enough new birds to put us over our 50-species goal. Highlights were a Wilson's Phalarope and three Bullock's Orioles. Final total for Utah stood at 58. Chalked up another state! That would be our 28th. Twenty-two to go.

We stopped at Dinosaur National Monument and checked out the quarry. Very impressive. Something like 1600 bones are visible in the indoor slab. Stopped in Craig for a KFC fix for lunch. My cholesterol was down a quart.

Got to Steamboat Springs and checked into the Days Inn. It was pretty crappy. No soap in the bathroom. Dirty floors. Yuck. We were going to go shopping at F.M. Light's, but we were too pooped to go back out. We needed some down time.

We saw an amusing sign along the road today: TWENTY MILE ROAD; Oak Creek→23 miles. I suppose you have to drive cross country the last three miles. Or you need an ATV of some sort.

We hit the road by about 5:30 the following morning and drove up Rte. 14 to Walden and Arapaho NWR. Along the way we saw a MOOSE(!) How cool was that? Arapaho was a wonderful NWR. Besides about 35 bird species we saw hundreds of Wyoming Ground Squirrels and Prairie Dogs as well as a Badger. We drove Rte. 14 all the way to Fort Collins over the Rockies.

Road signs of the day:

## Icy Conditions May Exist

## Avalanche Conditions May Exist

These two, of course, reminded us of the possible existence of gusty winds in Albuquerque. Our favorite for the day, though, was:

## In Case of Flood Climb to Safety

This last sign was at the base of a cliff that reached up at least a couple of hundred feet. The other side of the road was the river. Not much chance to climb to safety.

Lunch was at Bennigan's in Fort Collins. We checked into a Comfort Inn in Estes Park that afternoon. Sue did some laundry. We walked part way around Estes Lake – there were a lot of Elk in that town. Literally IN town.

We treated ourselves to a nice dinner in town. We realized at dinner that we BOTH forgot our anniversary *three days before*. Good thing we **BOTH** forgot! Guess we were too busy looking for birds in Idaho. Speaking of The Quest, we were comfortably over fifty species in Colorado, so we had swept all four states on the trip. 29 down, 21 to go. On our way to the car after dinner we spotted a sign in a shop window: "God invented whiskey to keep the Irish from ruling the world." I'll drink to that.

We got up about 6 the next morning and went for a short walk around Estes Lake again. We had a nice big breakfast at The Egg and I before heading into Rocky Mountain National Park.

Hiking the Cub Lake Trail, we saw some nice birds – Red-naped Sapsucker comes to mind – as well as hundreds of Elk.

It was snowing toward the end and our energy was flagging. We drove around and walked a bit at Sprague Lake. Drove up to Bear Lake and it was cold, the trail was icy, and we decided simply to head out. We never did find a Gray Jay or any of the high-altitude birds we had hoped for. We were, however, well over 50 Colorado birds so we decided to return to Denver and see about moving our departure up a couple of days.

We stopped at Two Ponds NWR – a modest refuge at most – before going to the airport. You may recall that we tried visiting near the beginning of this trip, but it was closed. This time it was open, but we only managed to find twelve species of birds and none of them added to our Colorado list. Alas.

# Chapter 16
## Michigan, Wisconsin, and extras for Illinois
### Sunday, May 22 – Tuesday, May 31, 2005

Happy Birthday, Dear Susan, Happy Birthday to you. We left home about seven. Stopped in Morgantown for gas at Sheetz and breakfast at Mickey D's. Spent most of the rest of the day driving to Port Clinton, OH. Or possibly Portage. In any case, we stayed at a Sleep Inn in one of those places that starts with a "Port" on Rte. 53.

We had beautiful weather until just west of Cleveland. Stopped at the Marblehead Lighthouse, which was the oldest lighthouse in continuous operation on the Great Lakes. Since 1822 the beacon had been warning sailors to steer clear of the rocks of Marblehead Peninsula which were impressive indeed. During our visit it loomed comfortingly out of a foggy, drizzly morning. Some soggy birding there produced exactly twelve species of birds. Four of them were actually new for our Ohio list which had climbed to a whopping 55 species.

After getting thoroughly wet and somewhat chilled, we decided to get some dinner. A couple of miles up the road we found a winery/restaurant called "Mon Ami." Sue had chicken and broccoli, I had the shrimp special – a pound(!) of shrimp for eight bucks. It was actually more than I could eat. This does not happen very often. Burp.

We were up at 6 and had breakfast at Mickey D's before a bit of birding at Ottawa NWR. We got 31 species there (including several Indigo Buntings and lots of Dunlin) and probably added another handful to our previous 55 Ohio birds.

I missed the turn for Cedar Point NWR just east of Toledo, and rather than back-tracking (Sue taught me to hate that) we continued driving across central Michigan to Shiawasee NWR. The weather was rainy all morning, but we hiked a mile or more around the refuge and found about 36 species. Combined with our OTR (on the road) list, my current best guess was 45 birds for Michigan! Getting our 50 birds looked pretty certain. The next morning we were meeting up with a Kirtland's Warbler tour which promised to be rewarding

119

and fun. We went to a gift shop in Grayling and got pins and a patch. Now we just needed to get the bird...

We got up around 5:30 the next morning. Loaded the car and had breakfast in the restaurant at the Holiday Inn. At 7 we went to the Maple Room for our meeting with the USFG woman. She showed us an informative slide presentation about the Kirtland's Warbler and efforts to manage its habitat. We offered to drive an old(er) couple to the refuge so they could leave their dogs in their car. They were v e r y  s l o w. We were very gracious. So anyway, there were about eight people in the group.

We drove out to the NWR and yes, we got nice looks at two singing male Kirtland's Warblers, along with enough miscellaneous other species to pass our 50-bird goal. That made Michigan the 30th state completed in our Fifty Birds in Fifty States quest. Hooray.

We dropped off Herb and Pat (the old folks) back in Grayling and headed north to Seney. We hiked the nature trail and drove the auto route around Seney NWR. Highlights there were Sandhill Cranes and nesting Trumpeter Swans. A LOT of Trumpeter Swans.

Sue thought Grand Marais would offer more choices of motels and restaurants than Seney, so we drove up there. However, Grand Marais was as bleak as Germfask and Seney. We ended up at the Fox River Inn (or some such) in Seney. $38 a night! Seriously. And it was clean. We weren't sure about the lock on our door, but the price was right and we suspected there was less of a criminal element there than say, back in Philadelphia. We were only ten minutes or so from the NWR. In fact, we drove around it again at dusk and saw lots more swans, a muskrat and a couple of beavers. Dinner that night was at a local restaurant. The one that was open. It was acceptable. Nuff said.

We had a light breakfast of granola bars and fruit in our room and got to Seney NWR around 6:30 the following morning. We walked the nature trail again and found about 28 species along it. We heard a number of American Bitterns

120

booming in the marsh. 'Way cool. We also drove the auto route and saw a lot of (maybe a hundred?) Trumpeter Swans displaying courtship behavior – head bobbing and wing flapping and, um, er, ah, trumpeting.

When we stopped back at the visitor's center we were chatting with one of the volunteers who was a retired band director from a Chicago-area high school. He offered to give us his spiel and show us the slide presentation about the refuge. Both were very interesting and well-done.

The rest of the day was spent driving across the Upper Peninsula. Miles and miles and miles of not much. We were beginning to think it was infinite just before we finally reached Wisconsin. Drove all the way to Ashland and went up Route 13 looking for the Whittlesy Creek NWR. When we got to Washburn, we realized we had gone too far. We checked into a Motel 8 in Washburn.

Then we drove back down to Ashland and found the Visitor's Center. Had a nice visit with a woman ranger and walked the nature trail. It was drizzling, but we found a few new Wisconsin birds – Black-and-white Warbler and Great Crested Flycatcher were the most interesting. We planned to visit there again in the morning before heading south to Horicon Marsh. We had a nice dinner at the Deep Water microbrewery/restaurant in Ashland.

Woke up early and hit the road by 6:30. Skipped a return to Wittlesy Creek. The drive for the day was over 300 miles, but seemed less deadly dull than yesterday, perhaps because we were fresher.

In any case, we got to Horicon about 12:30 and drove around some of the refuge. This marsh was one of Roger Tory Peterson's twelve favorite birding spots in the U.S. We managed to find 50 species there – we had a total of 71 birds for Wisconsin by my then-current guesstimate

We decided to check out the Mayville Inn right next to the refuge. It was a lovely place and the owner (Jane) was very helpful with suggestions of good places to look for birds. In fact, she gave us a better map than we got at the NWR visitor's center. Oh, and she recommended a range of restaurants from basic to hoity-toity. We opted for basic and had a nice dinner at Roxy's before hiking one of the trails at the refuge. We saw at least thirty Black Terns, some Redheads, Yellow-headed Blackbirds, and lots more. We were very tired that evening for some reason…

Imaginary bumper sticker for today: **I CUT THE CHEESE IN WISCONSIN**

We were ready to leave the Mayville Inn by about 5:50 next morning. Jane insisted we have some breakfast. We still got to our first hiking trail at Horicon Marsh by 6:30 or so. Saw a male Turkey displaying for four females along the way. We chatted with a couple of other birders along the floating boardwalk. The second fellow helped us find a Sora. He also pointed out an Eagle's nest (with Eagles, of course.) We had fifty species by 8 AM and toyed with going for a "big day."

Unfortunately, we ran out of steam, so we decided to drive to the Nachusa Grasslands in Illinois.

Unfortunately, when we got to Route 33, I asked Sue whether to go east or west. She said "east." We shoulda gone west.

Unfortunately, by the time we realized our mistake, we were nearly to Milwaukee!

Unfortunately, we decided to try for Little Gulls in Manitowoc, based on a book published in 1996.

Unfortunately, when we got to the place described in the book there was a fellow with a twelve-gauge shotgun SHOOTING GULLS FROM THE JETTY!!!! Whiskey. Tango. Foxtrot.

Fortunately, we decided to throw in the towel. We called Sue's sister and brother-in-law on the car phone (imagine two old farts talking to the roof of an SUV.) So we drove to their house in Evanston and they fed us and we crashed for the night.

We took it easy the following day. Breakfast was around 9. Then we went into town and Rick and I wandered around

Bookman's Alley while Sue and Paula were ordering frames for pictures Paula had purchased on a recent trip to China.

We got up around 5 AM CDT next morning. No, wait. We were on the road by 5 AM, we got up around 4. It would have been 5 at home. I think. Spent the day driving all the way home. The weather was beautiful and traffic wasn't outrageous. The drive took about thirteen and a half hours.

A couple of days later, I finished putting the birds from the trip into our database. Final totals: Michigan 73 species; Wisconsin 87; and Illinois jumped from 62 to 73.

## Chapter 17
## South Dakota, Wyoming, Montana, Minnesota
## Wednesday, July 27 – Friday, August 12, 2005

There were times when we interwove our quest for Fifty Birds in Fifty States into the fabric of other activities. At the end of July 2005 we had been invited to attend the wedding of Sue's niece, Heather, in Chicago. It was just a couple of days before we were scheduled to participate in an Elderhostel program in Yellowstone National Park, so we decided to drive all the way out and back. While loading the car for the trip I tweaked something in my back, so most of the ride was a very painful experience.

The first day out we drove from our home in Coatesville all the way to a Holiday Inn Express in Ohio about thirty miles from the eastern border of Indiana. We arrived there around 6 after driving about nine hours. There was a restaurant across the road called "Smith's," and Sue had a "tough but tasty" rib eye and I had "pig wings" – pork chops with Buffalo wing seasoning. Our room had a jacuzzi, so we took turns unwinding. It made the pain in my back ease a little. Then we watched the Yankees play the Twins. Johann Santana was pitching for the Twins, Al Leiter for the Yanks. That may be more information than you want to know...

We had a 5:30 wake-up in the morning. We were on the road by 6:30. Stopped at Harrison Lake State Park at exit 25 of the Ohio Turnpike. Saw some nice birds. Stuff like Belted Kingfishers, Cedar Waxwings and quite a few more common species.
Then we got back on the turnpike and headed to Chicago. I drove the first leg to South Bend, Indiana. We stopped there for gas and changed drivers. We got to Evanston around 11 Eastern time. Stopped at our hotel forgetting we were in the Central time zone. duh.

So we went over to Paula and Rick's (Sue 's sister and brother-in-law) and visited and had some lunch. Went back to the hotel for a short nap. Then we walked to CVS and got some "Icy Hot" patches for my back. And some for Sue's aching shoulder.

We got up fairly late – around 7:30 or 8 – the next morning. Had a big breakfast at Le Peep. Then we went for a walk at Northwestern University – the "lake fill." Saw about 18 species. Main event for the day was the wedding of Sue's niece, Heather. Got to meet the groom's family and some of Rick's folks. The groom was a Reagan Republican, so I wondered how this was going to work out…[It didn't.]

The following day we drove about 880 miles. Seriously. We got up at 4:30 and left the hotel at 5:11. We hit I-90 west of Skokie and drove across Illinois, Wisconsin, Minnesota and South Dakota. Traffic wasn't bad and other than the boredom factor, it was a good drive. We stopped at a rest area on the east bank of the Missouri River and took some pictures. There was a Lewis and Clark exhibit there that was modest but interesting. It included a replica of one of the boats they used in navigating up the Missouri as well as other some artifacts. All were accompanied by appropriate explanatory plaques, of course. The temperature at the stop was 103° F according to the thermometer in Sue's car. The highest temperature I noticed that afternoon was 104°.

As we approached Wall, South Dakota, there was a thunderstorm coming at us from the west and it provided some dramatic skies – curtains of gray rain illuminated by jagged lines of lightning. At one point we passed a prairie fire evidently touched off by the lightning. There were several fire trucks there when we passed, although it seemed as if the rain would have extinguished it pretty quickly. After we checked into our motel, we walked over to the famous Wall Drugs and

125

got a bite to eat. We actually bought some souvenirs and hats. NOT at Wall Drug, but across the street where they were cheaper. We saw a Western Kingbird and a Common Nighthawk in town while wandering around. There may have been two Nighthawks, but we never saw both of them at once, so it was impossible to say for sure.

We got our 5 am wake-up call the next morning as promised. Hit the road by about ten of six. Drove from Wall Drug to Rapid City and down to Mount Rushmore. Stopped briefly to take pictures from various angles (of the presidents, of course.) There was a small group of Mountain Goats near the visitor's center. Next we headed over to Deadwood, where we made a pilgrimage to the graves of Wild Bill Hickock and Calamity Jane. There was a Least Chipmunk scurrying around among the gravestones.

Continued back to I-90 and the serious business of driving to Montana.

We were scheduled to register for our Elderhostel program between 4 and 5. Actually got to Rte. 89 in Livingston about 3:25, so we had plenty of time to get there. Despite the crappy directions from Elderhostel, we found it without much trouble. There were 21 participants in our group. A good number of them were birders and perhaps half of us had never been to Yellowstone before. Our "Weed Warrior" instructor/leader was Linda W, a long-time Yellowstone volunteer. The Elderhostel coordinator was Dorothy Ann ("D.A.") H – a very sweet octogenarian who seemed to have things well in hand. Dinner was rainbow trout and veggies.

Orientation after dinner was reasonably brief and to the point – we were introduced to our enemies for the week: Mullein, Dalmatian Toadflax, Hound's Tongue and Spotted Knapweed. I still think Dalmatian Toadflax sounds like an ingredient for a wizard's potion

126

in a Harry Potter story. Now that I think about it, Hound's Tongue and Spotted Knapweed do too.

The place we were staying was called Beede's Resort. It was a series of log cabins along the Yellowstone River and a large central building that housed a dining/meeting room. Our cabin was roomy, clean and comfortable. There were a few interesting birds near the "resort" including a pair of nesting Ospreys and a number of Violet-green Swallows.

In case we needed a reminder that we were in a very conservative area of the country, there was a sign painted on a barn in Corwin Springs, MT:

**Clinton Don't Inhale. He Sucks**.

The following day was the first of work on our service project, "Weeding Yellowstone." The bus ride to our work area took over an hour. Closer to two hours, in fact. The beginning was inauspicious when we came to a bridge marked "Safe for 11 Tons" and our driver determined that the unloaded weight of our vehicle was 26,000 pounds. We all got off and walked across the bridge. It did not collapse under the bus. We would take a different route the following day.

Most of the morning was spent in digging and pulling out Dalmatian Toadflax. We worked along the Madison River and with 21 of us along we removed several thousand plants that day.

We had a picnic lunch along the river and put in another hour of weeding after lunch. I found and removed a patch of Mullein with a total of 31 plants in it. Most of them were first-year rosettes. This was a nice way to see Yellowstone in the summer. We were mostly working away from the swarms of tourists, many of whom seemed to be complete idiots. Shocking, I know, but painfully true. The food there was good and the group was congenial.

Work time the next morning was spent weeding at the Heritage Center. It was a massive job, but we got good results. I took some pictures of the piles of weeds we left on the sidewalk. Around 10:45 we knocked off work for the day and made an excursion to the Boiling River. This involved a short bus trip followed by about a half-mile hike. Soaking in the river was a unique experience. The water in the Gardiner River was icy cold. The water from the Boiling River was, well, boiling hot. No, really. So we could sit with cold water bathing our feet and bottoms while hot water washed over our shoulders and backs. It felt good after all of the physical activity.

We had lunch back at Beede's Resort, followed by a wildlife lecture by Gene B. He showed slides and told stories. I would give him a B- for his presentation, to be honest. The professor in me never sleeps. After the talk we got back on our bus for an excursion to the Lamar Valley to actually look for wildlife. It was not the best time of year, but we did see more than 100 Bison, 6-8 Mule Deer, 3 Coyotes, 2 Prairie Falcons, 5-6 Ospreys and a Uinta Ground Squirrel.

At one of our potty stops, I visited a souvenir shop and found the perfect kitsch item. Maybe my best of all time. Are you ready for this? A BOBBLEHEAD BISON. I am not making that up. We got back to the resort around 9:30 this evening, tired but pooped. Too much fun today. Again.

Before I forget, Gene told endless stories on the bus trip. Two come to mind:

"A couple of women were getting ready to take their first back country hike. They kept calling their outfitter to ask whether they needed this or that until he finally said, 'Look. You two just come in with your underwear and your credit cards and I will sell you everything you need.'"

128

"An ornithologist was explaining how to tell a Crow from a Raven. He explained that the Raven has 5 pinion feathers while the Crow has just 4. So it is simply a difference of a pinion." Go ahead. Groan.

(next evening) Phew. We had an exhausting day in paradise. After breakfast (scrambled eggs and sausage) we rode 60+ miles on the bus to the Old Faithful area of Yellowstone. We arrived around 10 and spent the next several hours hauling logs up from the riverbank to a pile near a maintenance shed. These were the remains of an old mule corral. The Park Service didn't want to take heavy equipment in and kill the native plants they were trying to re-establish. Hence, slave labor. Oh, and we had to knock apart numerous pieces that were fastened together with railroad spikes. Pretty intense. Dale P and I did most of the sledgehammer work. Took me back to my youth on the farm. Of course in those days my body was less apt to scream at me for two days afterwards.

We had our picnic lunch at the work site and then worked some more until about 2 in the afternoon. Our next stop was at Old Faithful where we had considerable free time to visit shops and the like. Sue and I made a stop at the Bear Pit Restaurant for a drink. We witnessed three separate eruptions of the geyser (the first was pretty lame) and ate our dinner in the cafeteria at Old Faithful Lodge. We didn't get "home" until nearly 9:30 again. G'night.

After breakfast the following morning we drove to the Mammoth Hot Springs area where half of the group (our half) went on a five-mile hike along the Beaver Pond Trail with Paul M, a long-time ranger at Yellowstone. Paul was very soft-spoken and reminded us all of a sixties hippy caught in a time warp. Along the trail we disposed of Dalmatian Toadflax, Hound's Tongue and occasional Spotted Knapweed. The Hound's Tongue was all packed in large garbage bags and hauled out by volunteers. That would be us. I think it was to be cremated later in a quiet, out-of-the way place. Probably without ceremony.

At one point in the morning, Paul took us "off trail" to see a wikiup built by the Sheepeater Shoshone who lived there. We pointed out that Gene B told us a couple of days ago that there was no evidence that Indians ever resided in the park. Paul promised to enlighten Gene when he sees him. He even wrote Gene's name on the palm of his hand as a reminder.

During another break Paul told a Shaggy Dog story about how the Douglas Fir got its name. It involved ancient mice who buried their dead in the cones – you can still see their little hind feet sticking out. Yeah.

The hike lasted (with breaks and a picnic lunch, of course) until around 3 PM. Everyone was tired. We saw some nice birds along the way, including several Clark's Nutcrackers and a male Western Tanager. Oh, and there was an Otter at one of the Beaver ponds. After supper tonight Linda W (our main guide) did a little presentation on wildflowers found in Yellowstone. More important, she introduced us to Moose Drool beer. It tasted much better than it sounded…

On the last day of the Elderhostel, we destroyed a patch of Mullein and some scattered Knapweed around the Mammoth Hot Springs in the morning. That was our last work assignment for the program. At one point a couple of tourists stopped and asked what we were doing. They thanked us profusely for doing such a wonderful public service. Um, yeah, sure.

We spent the rest of the day visiting the Grand Canyon of Yellowstone, the Upper and Lower Falls, and the Hayden Valley. Hundreds, maybe thousands, of rutting Bison being admired by thousands of stupid tourists, some of whom seemed to be looking for ways to be eliminated from the gene pool. The rest of us should be so lucky.

When we got back to Gardiner, nine of the group (including Yours Truly) took a raft trip down the Yellowstone River past our cabins. We had a great time and our last dinner together was very cordial. What a wonderful week! Did I mention that we finally spotted some Gray Jays during our lunch break that last afternoon? No? How about the BLACK BEAR I finally saw from the bus on the way back? He was huge. Unless it was a she. How cool was that?

We got up around 5:25 and hit the road before six. Shelly had left us muffins for our breakfast, and I got a cup of coffee to take along, too. We stopped at the old Roosevelt Arch and took some pictures. Got ice for our cooler at Mammoth Hot Springs and drove on to Yellowstone Lake, where we had breakfast around 8:10 at Lake Lodge. Worked our way out of the park through numerous Bison jams and construction delays.

Proceeded to Cody, where we spent some time at the Buffalo Bill History Center (and the art galleries.) Then we found a car wash and neighboring laundromat. While Sue worked on doing laundry, I walked over to Paul and Beth's Café and got sandwiches and soft drinks for lunch.

We checked into Buffalo Bill's Original Irma Hotel (named for his daughter.) Walked around town – mostly souvenir shops and hunting and fishing outfitters. We went back to the Natural History Museum at Buffalo Bill's History Center, where I learned that the Mountain Goats in the Rockies were introduced for hunting. Isn't wildlife there so we can kill it?

We returned to the Irma in time for the daily gunfight re-enactment. It was pretty lame, but they did it to raise money for charity. We ate dinner in the Irma's lounge. The crowd was dominated by bikers, since this is the time of year when there was a Harley rally in Sturgis, SD.

We had a wake-up call at the Irma at 5 the next morning. We drove out to Mentock Park to watch the Wild West Balloon Fest. When we got there, the guys were just arriving with their balloons, so we went back to Granny's for a big breakfast. Back at the park, there was a "weather delay" so we decided to hit the road.

We drove all the way to Devil's Tower. As we crossed the highest point (and stopped to let the car engine cool down) my GPS registered the elevation as 9492', although a sign along the road read only 9430'. Close enough. The density of Harley's had increased as the day wore on – the big rally officially started the following day. Devil's Tower was jammed with cars and hogs – Harley hogs, of course. We took NUMEROUS pictures of the tower, bought a patch for our banner and moved on.

We stopped for lunch at a Hardee's on the road and continued on to Custer. We found a Best Western for too much money and checked in. Driving down from Spearfish the Harleys were thicker than maggots on a gut wagon, as my Dad used to put it. We came up with a conservative estimate of 2500 bikes passing us each hour. Deadwood and Hill City were both wall-to-wall with bikes and bikers. According to ESPN, there were more than 700,000 bikers at the rally.

We passed a number of curious and/or humorous signs today:

> **Corbett's Shebang** [historical marker – no, we didn't stop to read it]
> **Bargins Unlimited** [in Ralston WY]
> **Aunt Tique and Uncle Junque** [a shop in Lovell, WY]
> **Alladdin Tipple** [Alladin, WY – pop. 15]

Breakfast was at the Wrangler Café in Custer the next morning because it was open at 6. We drove up to Crazy Horse Mountain and wandered around for an hour or so taking pictures and buying souvenirs. Next drove to the Badlands National Park and drove around the loop road. The landscapes looked like they were imported from Mars or the Moon or possibly an entirely different solar system.

Spent most of the rest of the day driving across South Dakota. We did make a brief stop in Mitchell to see the famous Corn Palace. Took the pictures. Bought the kitsch.

Then we made our way as far as Pipestone National Monument in Minnesota. We stopped there and hiked the modest nature trail. Saw some nice birds and neglected (both of us) to take our cameras along. We considered spending the night in Pipestone (the town, not the monument) but the only motel in town was a Super 8 that looked much too scruffy to take a chance on. So we continued on to Marshall. Got a nice room at the local AmericInn for about $110 less than last night in Custer. Ouch. Had a decent dinner at the local Applebee's.

We actually slept in until 7:30. Had breakfast at the hotel and got on the road about 8:30. Drove to St. Cloud and continued on to the Sherburne NWR. Checked out the Visitor's Center and the Wildlife Loop Drive and found 25 species or so. Planned to return next morning. Stopped in Foley and got an oil change, then returned to St. Cloud for a late lunch and got a room at the Country Inn and Suites. Soaked in the spa. Swam in the pool. Watched some TV. Wrote some postcards. Skipped dinner.

We were up by 5:30 and got to Sherburne NWR by 7 or so. Drove the loop and walked a couple of the trails. Got 44 species there. Called our friend Jane from the car to let her know we were getting close. We got to Mille Lacs a bit before 11. Visited with Jane and Doug until 3 or so and went back to our motel for a rest. Jane insisted on paying for our room. We had dinner with

133

them at a nice restaurant on the lake and I insisted on paying, so there. Walking by the lake we were impressed with the enormous clouds of "Mayflies". Wow. The flies in huge numbers made a humming/buzzing reminiscent of truck tires on the interstate.

We spent another quiet and pleasant day with Doug and Jane. Met them at Pat's Restaurant in the town of Isle for breakfast. Then Jane and Sue ran some errands while Doug and I went back to their cabin. Sat on the dock. Wandered a bit in the woods. When Jane and Sue returned, Doug and I went to pick up their mail and I identified several birds for him on his favorite walking trail. Sue and I went out on the lake in their canoe for an hour or so. Saw a handful of birds, including a few Redheads (new for MN). I did a count of our Minnesota birds that morning and got a total of 60. State #32 completed.

We hit the road around ten 'til six .Drove until about 7:10 and pulled into a Perkins for breakfast. The car phone rang as we stopped in the parking lot. It was my son, Todd, calling to tell us that our new grandson, Colin James arrived at 1:11 PM the day before. Exciting news! Breakfast was slow arriving, but tasty.

Back on the road until we took a late lunch around 1:30 in Edgerton, WI. Along the way near Turtle Creek, WI, we passed a number of streets with fractional numbers – as in "1½ Street and 3¼ Street and my favorite, 8¾ Street." How do you pronounce that one? Eight and three quarterth Street? Oh well. The restaurant where we stopped was pretty grubby looking, but the food was good. Then back to driving. Chicago was congested and there was a lot of construction (with delays, of course) around the Indiana border. Tomorrow, HOME!

# Chapter 18
## Nevada and a return to Utah
### Thursday, September 22 – Tuesday, October 4, 2005

When we landed in Las Vegas around 10 AM local time, the weather was sunny and warm. Hot, even. Ah, Vegas. Slot machines in the airport. Slot machines in motels. Slot machines everywhere you go. I swear there were even slot machines in the rest rooms. Yawn.

We drove to Pahrump, about 53 miles west of Vegas. As in "Come, they told me pahrumpapumpum." Checked into a Best Western and ate lunch at the restaurant there. As planned, we drove over to Ash Meadows NWR another thirty miles or so west. It was mid-afternoon, so there were not a lot of birds out, but we did see some nice ones - Crissal Thrasher comes to mind. On our way out of the refuge we saw a Greater Roadrunner and a flock of Gambel's Quail. If we ever get tired of seeing either of those critters, just take us out behind the barn and shoot us.

We got back to Pahrump around five. Got some food (yoghurt, fruit, trail mix) at the local Albertson's as well as a case of bottled water. Did I mention that there are slot machines in grocery stores here?

In addition to today's birds, Sue saw a Coyote. We both saw a Desert Cottontail and 3-4 Side-blotched Lizards. That is what the rangers said they are called. There were also some ground squirrels or chipmunks running across the road in a couple of places. Fleeting glimpses would have been an improvement.

We got up early the following morning and were on the road by about five after six. Drove to Pahranagat NWR after a slight delay when we went past the last gas station and decided it would be prudent to drive back. Out in the desert it is best to err on the safe side. We did see some nice birds at Pahranagat - scads of Gambel's Quail (which we still enjoyed seeing – not

135

time to shoot us yet) as well as a Black-headed Grosbeak and another Roadrunner. Also saw a biggish lizard and I tried to catch a picture of him, but what I got was a beautiful shot of the prickly pear he was hiding behind.

Anyway, we spent the rest of the day driving up to Ely, where we found there was a rodeo and a car race going on that weekend. We had to try three motels before we found a room available. It was a Best Western, so we would get credit towards our rewards, whatever they might be. Probably free nights at another Best Western. At one point along Rte. 93 a herd of cattle held us up for fifteen or twenty minutes. A cowgirl finally came along on her horse and made a break for us to drive through. A late lunch at a local Mexican restaurant was decent. Visits to Comins Lake and Cave Lake State Park were disappointing. Got a few birds at Comins, nothing whatsoever at Cave Lake. Wrong time of day and all that.

The McDonald's in Ely had a sign out front saying that they started serving at 5:30. We got there around 5:25 and there was one guy working in the back. We went across the road and got some breakfast items at a convenience store. By the time we hit the road to Great Basin National Park, Mickey D's was still not open.

We got to Great Basin National Park by just before 7. We stopped at several places along the road to look for birds. Walked part of the trail at Osceola Ditch and saw a Clark's Nutcracker and several Mountain Chickadees and White-breasted Nuthatches. We drove up the Wheeler Peak Scenic Drive (or whatever it was called) and hiked a short trail up there. Not many birds about other than Ravens and an occasional Flicker. Drove back down the mountain and stopped at the visitors' center to get patches and pins at the gift shop.

Went back down to Baker and checked out the "Baker Archaeological Site." It was basically the ruins of a 700-year-old Indian settlement. There were quite a few Horned Larks flying about the fields. We got up to 47 Nevada birds and figured we could get our last three after the Elderhostel in Utah was over.

So we drove from Baker, NV to Cedar City, UT that afternoon. There was a Shakespeare Festival going on as well as some sort of county celebration. We managed to find a hotel room at a Best Western before traffic was pretty much stopped for a parade. We walked over to Gandolfo's New York Deli for a sandwich. I checked out the local bookstore and bought a *Naturalist's Guide to Canyon Country*. The bookstore had an entire rack of greeting cards to send to missionaries. Seriously. There was a whole wall of shelves devoted to "LDS Fiction" - which did not, for some reason, include the Book of Mormon. I am so naughty.

We watched a bit of the parade. The marching band from Southern Utah University didn't totally suck. They were dressed in bright red uniforms with old-fashioned tall hats with tassels. Red seemed to be the color of the day. The University Democrats consisted of a young lady driving a pickup truck. She wasn't booed, at least. The university president drove by with his wife (and a driver, of course) in a Model A convertible. The parade lasted quite a while. We walked over to the Art Festival, which wasn't much. I know, I know. I sound like an East Coast Snob. Deal with it.

First stop the next day was Cedar Breaks National Monument. The visitors' center was at around 10,000 feet elevation. It was very cold up there - in the high thirties. We took lots of pictures from various overlooks. The rock formations were spectacular, colorful, dramatic. Wow, even.

We hiked the trail to the Alpine Lake. Saw a few birds, including a Prairie Falcon. Next destination was

Zion National Park. Talk about dramatic scenery! Steep roads. Switchbacks. Tunnels. Bizarre rock formations. We drove from there to St. George, UT where we would be based for a couple of days. Had some lunch at a Holiday Inn restaurant (the Palms) and walked around the "historic district" of St. George. I suspected it was historic because most of the businesses down there were "history." There were a lot of empty store fronts. Pretty depressed and depressing.

We stopped at the Blue Bunny for ice cream. Before you say a word, they had no-sugar low-fat ice cream and that's what I got. So there. Went back to the Elderhostel place where we were staying (part of Dixie State College) and spent some time swimming and lounging around the pool. Watched some baseball on TV and got the results from back home. The Phillies won and so did the Eagles that day. Yay Philly. We have met some of the other participants. One couple came in on the Las Vegas shuttle thinking that the program started that day. We helped them get hold of someone who found them a room in the dorm.

As a consequence of Sue's philosophy that "a clean car is a happy car," the next morning we stopped at a car wash in St. George and, well, had the car washed. Most of the fellows finishing up with the wiping down stage looked Mexican. I was watching one of them as he worked on a white Thunderbird. He was a skinny guy with a thin mustache, maybe twenty-five years old. He first stopped one nostril and blew his nose on the ground farmer fashion. Then (I am NOT making this up!) He BLEW HIS NOSE ON THE RAG HE USED TO WIPE DOWN THE CAR! Jeez Louise. I'm thinking not all clean cars are happy cars.

We decided to check out Snow Canyon State Park, which was about five miles from downtown St. George. What a wonderful bit of luck! Snow Canyon (named for a Mormon pioneer, or possibly two of them) was gorgeous. Sandstone cliffs. Petrified sand dunes.

138

Desert varnish. Basalt flows. Stunning scenery at every turn. We walked a shortish trail called "Pioneer Names." It was called that because several late-nineteenth century pioneers wrote their names on the rocks in axle grease from their wagons. So over a hundred years later, they are still there in the desert. Today it would be called vandalism. What a difference a hundred-year perspective makes. As we hiked we could hear Rock Pigeons cooing in the caves high up on the cliffs. The echoes made the sound haunting and beautiful.

Next we hiked a longish trail (a couple of miles) called the Hidden Pinyon Trail. I chose it because the park brochure said it had markers pointing out interesting plants and geological features. The plants included Mormon Tea and Creosote Bushes among others. The geological features encompassed the aforementioned Desert Varnish (probably caused by microorganisms depositing manganese and iron on the rocks) as well as various sedimentary and volcanic rock formations. Along the way we saw a couple of Rock Wrens and a Spotted Towhee, a few Rock Squirrels, several Northern Whiptails and, um, er, a Black-tailed Gnatcatcher.

Lunch today was at a local JB's. We came back to the Dixie College Inn and spent an hour lounging around the pool and even swimming a bit. At three we registered officially with the Elderhostel. At 4:15 we had an orientation meeting. To tell the truth the leaders seemed a bit disorganized, but we figured it would probably work out OK. Dinner was at the college cafeteria. It was simple but tasty.

We had a "class" with Lin Alder, one of our instructors for the week, at seven o'clock. He seemed knowledgeable and pleasant. We chatted with a number of others at dinner and after class and the company seemed interesting and stimulating. I neglected to mention that the theme of this Elderhostel program was digital photography.

Breakfast in the lobby of the Dixie College Inn was followed by a two-hour history lesson with a Dr. Alder who was the former president of the college. Also Lin's father. Elder Alder. He was an outstanding teacher and the class was surprisingly entertaining. We spent the second hour visiting the tabernacle and the courthouse. Then we had a second class with Tony Something. It was OK, but neither particularly well-organized nor engaging. In fact, I have forgotten his topic. Not a good sign. Yawn. Lunch was at Chuck-a-Rama – a big buffet place with enough choice to please nearly anybody. We made a brief stop at the Inn to get our luggage and spent the rest of the afternoon driving to the North Rim of the Grand Canyon.

During the drive, Lin and Q, our photography instructors covered lots of information about shutter speed, apertures, ISO settings and the like. I had no idea what they were talking about. We ran into some rain that was occasionally heavy on the way and after we arrived. Some of the hostile elders in this Elderhostel were rude and annoying. The group was simply too large. Folks were cranky after the long drive, but they didn't need to be jerks about it. Dinner was at the Lodge. The menu was pretty fancy schmancy and we had a good meal. Then we walked along the rim and took tons of sunset photos - Sue's camera batteries died. We did get some nice shots, though.

The following day started with photo shooting at the Grand Canyon at sunrise. We got more good pictures and saw a few birds that morning. Breakfast was at the lodge. After breakfast we still had nearly two hours before the bus was scheduled to leave, so we hiked around taking more pictures and finding a few more birds.

The bus was all loaded and left promptly at 10:30. We stopped just outside the park for a photo shoot at a stand of aspen trees. I accidentally left my camera on the bus, so I just wandered around looking interested. It was a pretty spot. Sue actually took some excellent pictures. Folks were experimenting with inventive angles, some even lying on the ground under trees and shooting up the trunks.

We stopped for lunch at a Chinese restaurant along the way to Zion. Lin and Q had managed to misplace my memory stick, but found it just as we stopped for lunch. Phew. The bus actually entered the canyon from the same road we took when we drove through on Sunday. The scenery was so spectacular that our brains got numb after a while.

We stayed at the Best Western in Springdale. Very nice. We had an early dinner so we could go out to the Weeping Rock for a photo shoot. My dinner was cold fish and chips. Enough said. The Weeping Rock was pretty and I guess the idea was to force us to figure out how to use low light. Very low light. I took some very bad pictures, but saw a number of Western Pipistrelles which compensated for the mediocre photography. Sue and I also saw a couple of Mule Deer. Came back to the hotel after dark and started editing our pictures. I was so tired I forgot to write this until Thursday morning. I lost my notebook with my bird notes and such, so I wrote up the day the best I could remember.

Guess what we were doing in Zion National Park? Taking lots and lots of pictures. I took something like 150 shots - more than half of which were total crap. We went out before sunrise and did some shooting around the museum. Then back to the motel for a breakfast buffet.

Returned to the park where we took the shuttle bus to the Temple of Sinawava and hiked the trail (ca. 1 mile each way.) Lots of goddam beautiful scenery. I actually got a couple of nice shots. We spotted two turkeys on the way into the park. Sue and I left the main group around eleven and took the shuttle to the Visitor's Center. We found our patch and pins and

141

bought extra batteries for our cameras. I also picked up the *Roadside Geology of Utah*. The book, not the entire geology.

We went back to the motel for another mediocre meal and then had some free time until 2. We ended up editing and weeding out our pictures and picking a couple for the group "class." We boarded the bus again around 5 and drove to the Kolob Canyon part of the park. Had box lunches. Well, brown bag dinners. Anyway, we ate them at the top of the road where there were wonderful views and no picnic tables. Of course, eating first wasted a lot of good light... Never mind.

Did I mention the size of some of the egos on this trip? Don't get me started. There were perhaps three diehards who would not board the bus that evening until the last photon disappeared behind the mountains. What they were photographing in the dark, I cannot imagine. I did take a shot of Perry A's butt crack which I offered to the group as "Moonflower". At least it got a laugh.

Breakfast at the Best Western in Springdale. It was a buffet. It was OK. Then we drove to the Zion Lodge parking area and hiked to the Emerald Pools. Took tons of pictures. We were supposed to "make" a picture today rather than "take" it. On the trail was a cement mixer for making trail repairs. Sue pretended to be barfing into it. I called the picture "Altitude Sickness." Later on I noticed some footprints in the concrete and had Ron E stand with his feet in two of them and photographed him so the prints behind him led up to his feet. I called that one "Dinosaur Tracks." Got a lot of laughs at the slide show this afternoon. Those people needed to lighten up, already.

Ron E was a band director who had actually worked with some of my former students. Ron's claim to fame was that he traveled around the country impersonating John Philip Sousa, complete with gaudy nineteenth-century uniform. Why not?

There was a particularly annoying pair of New Yorkers - we'll call them Bawbi and Mahty Oblivious. Bawbi held everyone up for thirty-five minutes one morning sitting on some goddam trail just out of sight of the bus. Her watch had stopped and she didn't notice! She was an idiot. Later in the day we all got to wait while Mahty took a crap. That old Western saying came to mind. "Some folks need to be killed."

After we "found" Bawbi the group drove to Bryce Canyon National Park. Had our daily slide show. Ate supper at the buffet. Took more pictures at Sunset Point. Well, in that general area. On our way through Zion before lunch we saw three Bighorn Sheep clinging to a mountainside. Very cool. Lots of Mule Deer and a herd of Pronghorns at one point.

The group drove out to Bryce Point for sunrise in the morning. I decided to walk the trail below the parking lot instead of joining the mobs who dutifully trekked out to the point. As a result I had a large area all to myself and a different viewpoint for my pictures. Oh, and it was quiet except for the birds and chipmunks. Got some nice shots.

Back to Ruby's Inn for breakfast. Sue and I skipped the next schlep out to the rim and stayed in our room downloading and editing pictures. We did get back on the bus when the group left around 10:45 to go to the Visitor's Center. Most of the folks went in to watch the film about Bryce. We went birding along one of the nearby trails. Saw lots of Western Bluebirds, a couple of Red-breasted Nuthatches, and best of all, a female Red Crossbill! That would be a life bird for both of us in North America.

Lunch at Ruby's Inn was followed by the drive back to St. George. We made one short stop for pix at Red Canyon. Well, and another short stop to pee. Back at Dixie State College we had our daily picture review followed by a slide show of pictures of people from the trip. There was a lot of laughter. I was "volunteered" to

143

organize a group to burn CDs for everyone. We think we may have participated in the first-ever CD-burning Bee in history.

Breakfast with the Elderhostel group at Dixie State College Inn Saturday morning was preceded by a surprise wake-up call when someone tried to toast a bagel and it caught fire. That set off the alarm system for the entire building. Got the adrenalin flowing, I'll give them that.

On the road by about eight Utah time, we drove down I-15 from St. George and took a detour to see Lake Mead. The bad news is that unless you have a boat there seems to be little reason to visit the lake. The good news is that we stopped at one of the oases formed by springs along the way and found a Black Phoebe. That along with a flock of Wild Turkeys, an Osprey and a Golden Eagle put us safely over our fifty-species goal for Nevada.

We took Rte. 95 northwest of Las Vegas all the way to Rte. 160, which took us back to Pahrump. It was not a town we wanted to live in. Dusty. Hot. Economically depressed-looking. We stopped at Indian Springs Casino and Restaurant for lunch. The place was pretty dirty, but the chicken wraps were OK. No, we didn't waste a cent on the penny slots.

We went back to the Best Western in Pahrump and checked the baseball and football scores. We drove out to Ash Meadows NWR again. It was very windy that afternoon, so we saw very few birds. It was still a pretty drive and a nice hike around the nature trail. We stopped at Albertson's and got some fruit for supper. We were both tired of eating – they seem to always overfeed us on Elderhostels. I just did a bird count and came up with 53 species for Nevada. In any case, I think we are safe to assume we have our fifty birds. Thirty-three states down, seventeen to go.

It was still very windy the next morning, so we decided to forego another drive out to Ash Meadows. Breakfast at the motel in Pahrump was followed by a drive to Hoover Dam. We didn't get a good look at the dam, and the area was very crowded, so we settled for a stop at the overlook on the lake side.

Lunch break in Boulder City was followed by a brief shopping walk. We got a patch for our banner and I picked up a coprolite at one of the rock shops. Fossilized dinosaur poop from Utah. I planned to put it in the kitsch cabinet.

That afternoon we drove back to Las Vegas and checked in to the Best Western near the airport. Returned our PT Cruiser (which we hated) to Dollar Rent-a-Car, which turned out to be just a block from our motel. Oh, before we did that we had dinner at an Italian place a mile or so down the road (String's.) Nice meal, and the food was HOT for a change. No more buffets for a while, please!

We had a wake-up call at 4 the next morning so we could catch the shuttle from the Best Western to the airport in Las Vegas. We got downstairs by about 4:40 or so, and the complete nitwit at the desk assured us that the shuttle would leave promptly at 5. He was rather snotty about it as a matter of fact. While waiting we chatted with a couple from Indiana. They had a 6:11 flight to catch and were getting a bit nervous. At 5:10 or so Sue went back inside to inquire what had happened to the driver. It seems he had overslept and the desk jerk had called a cab. Nice of him to tell us. He gave Sue $5 for the cab fare. It came to $5.70. Not that we are going to starve to death for the seventy cents, but the guy was so rude and obnoxious. I really should have complained to Best Western about all this, but I never did.

Anyway, we got to the airport in plenty of time and grabbed a bite to eat there. I had a fruit cup sort of thing that managed to make pineapple, cantaloupe and honeydew taste identical. Isn't modern technology wonderful? While Sue was having a smoke I noticed a pickup truck driving around the airfield with "DOA ESCORT" painted on the tailgate. Why a "DOA" would need an escort is still unclear. The plane took off nearly an hour late to accommodate passengers to Charlotte whose plane needed mechanical work. The flight was smooth, although the huge woman in front of me was a bit annoying. Every time she shifted her ample butt she popped my bottled water out of the seat pocket in front of me. I am not kidding. Anywho, we landed in Philly, got our car, stopped for cat food on the way home, paid the cat sitters, and started shifting through our junk mail.

# Chapter 19
## California Here We Come
### Wednesday, January 11 – Tuesday, January 17, 2006

In January of 2006 we flew out to California to participate in the Morro Bay Birding Festival. We had been invited by Perry and Louise A, a couple we had met on the photography Elderhostel in Utah. Louise was a birder. Perry was not particularly interested in birds, although he had come up with his own identification system. Tiny birds were all "sparrows." Medium-sized birds were mostly "pigeons." And large to very large birds were "chickens." It worked for him. His passion was glass blowing, a hobby for which we would be hard-pressed to come up with a meaningful vocabulary.

The drive up to Los Osos from the Los Angeles airport was not bad. Getting out of the car rental place was the hardest part. Sue clipped a pylon at the exit and we had to fill out all kinds of paperwork before we could actually head north. Along the way we did pass Buellton, "The Home of Split Pea Soup." Whatever that means. I don't think it was invented there. Too British. Oh yeah, along the way we saw seven or so species of birds. The ones we identified for sure were: Rock Pigeons, Starlings, Crows (all in the hundreds); at least nine Red-tailed Hawks, dozens of Turkey Vultures, at least 5 Kestrels, and a couple of Magpies, presumably Yellow-billed.

Perry and Louise had a lovely and large Lindal log home. We stayed in the "mother-in-law" suite, which was actually completely separate from the main house. We took them out to dinner at the Taco Temple. By about a quarter to eight we were totally exhausted, so we went to bed.

I thought I heard a Great-horned Owl or two during the night, but I could have dreamed it. We got up

147

around six. Perry knocked on our door around 6:40 and we joined him on his morning coffee shop excursion. Then we went back to the house for breakfast.

The rest of the morning involved driving north of Los Osos, past Cambria, to visit a colony of Elephant Seals not far from San Simeon. The pups were born at that time of year, and we saw a lot of babies – one of which had been born about fifteen minutes before we arrived. It was on the tag on his little wrist. Not really. The docent told us. The bulls were enormous and aggressive. The cows were less than half as big. The weather was sunny and mild. It was a perfect experience.

We stopped for lunch on our way back to Los Osos (The Bears) at a grill. The food was very tasty. We dropped Perry off at the house, and Louise drove us to Pismo to see a grove of eucalyptus that is a wintering place for Monarch butterflies. There were something like 20,000 butterflies there at the time according to a guide we talked to. There was also a little boy of about eight who seemed to think stomping the butterflies on the ground would be a fun thing to do. His ineffectual mother was asked to pick him up and leave the premises. I thought they should both be shot to get them out of the gene pool, but I guess that might be considered too extreme in some quarters. Even in California.

The four of us drove over to San Luis Obispo for dinner and a wander through the farmers' market. We saw a few more birds today, and I am guestimating that our CA count was around 25 species at that point. Halfway there.

The Great-horned Owl was not a dream yesterday, I heard it again and I was definitely awake. We got up around 5 and got over to the Birding Festival registration when they opened at 6. After checking in and getting our packets of information we had breakfast at Mickey D's. Then we stopped at Albertson's and got some granola bars, trail mix and bottled water.

Our first excursion of the day was "Birding multiple habitats at San Simeon State Park" or some such. The birding up there was really good, and we saw about 45 species, including several lifers for both of us. Snowy Plover, Nutall's Woodpecker, Chestnut-backed Chickadee, California Towhee, and Hutton's Vireo. To tell the truth, you have to be a bird nerd to get excited about Vireos. The whole family is made up of smallish gray birds with various yellow and/or white markings on their faces.

We had bag lunches which we ate on the return drive to Morro Bay. We got back about noon or noon thirty and our next group left at noon forty-five for the Botanical Gardens.

The Botanical Gardens were not too extensive, but the fellow who did our little tour was very nice, and we saw some good birds there - we got a great look at a Townsend's Warbler, for example. After dropping off the two ladies who had ridden with us from the Community Center, we went back to Perry and Louise's place and took a nap.

We returned to the Community Center for the reception that evening. We were tired, so we didn't stay very long. Sue bought a sculpture piece because we liked it and the price was very reasonable. Inexpensive even. After our nap, I did another rough estimate of our bird total for California and came up with 63 as a good guess. That was certainly in the ballpark, and it meant we had found fifty birds in 35 states - fifteen to go.

The weather was stinko the next morning, so our pelagic trip was cancelled. We expected as much, so we did not pine away over it. We decided to do some birding in Morro Bay State Park, and we found LOTS of good birds. We also drove over to Morro Rock where Sue took numerous pictures of the waves breaking over the jetty. We were glad not to be out on a boat in that swell. A Canyon Wren put on a little performance for us while we were there, and we saw a Hermit Thrush as well as a few Harbor Seals and Sea Otters.

Driving around to see where the Natural History Museum was, we passed a flock of Wild Turkeys. Very cool. Stopped at the museum for the "Birding from the Balcony" presentation. It was OK, but geared for beginners and we left after an hour. Then we drove out to Montana de Oro and ate our lunches in the car. Decided to drive up to San Simeon State Park and bird on our own.

We got maybe a quarter of a mile down the boardwalk before a drenching shower hit us. We got soaked (although there was a very intense rainbow across the park.) Went back to the house to dry out. We ate dinner with Jill and Perry and Louise. Jill made "the world's best meat loaf." It seemed pretty much like other meat loaf to me.

Speaking of Jill, I think I forgot to mention that she is another friend of Perry and Louise who was staying with them for the festival. She was a veterinarian, and I think she specialized in horses, although it could have been cats and dogs. She is one of those happily clumsy people who seem to break things by merely being in the same room with them. Things like a blown-glass mug that I'm sure Perry spent hours making. Louise, who is a computer guru of some sort, said that occasionally Jill checked out the stuff on her hard drive and started deleting any files she didn't recognize. Later she was puzzled when, for example, her computer refused to interact with her printer. Other than those two quirks, she seemed very bright and personable.

For our last activity of the day we drove over to the Morro Bay High School (Louise drove, actually) to hear Kenn Kauffman's talk about bird migration. It was pretty good, and he signed my field guide afterwards. Seemed like a pleasant chap, as a matter of fact.

We got up a bit later than usual, since our first expedition wasn't until 9:30. Had coffee and breakfast with Louise and Jill. Then we drove over to meet the group going to Morro Rock. The leader was the ranger who did the Birding from the Balcony activity yesterday. He talked about the difference between Sea Lions and Harbor Seals as well as explaining more than most wanted to know about various plumages in gulls. The Peregrine Falcons and the Canyon Wren made their appearances, as well as a couple of Harbor Seals and a Sea Otter. We slipped away after about an hour, because we had forgotten to get our lunches and we were getting hungry.

Went back to the Community Center and picked up our lunches, and I suggested we check out the Elfin Forest. We ate in the car before hiking the trails at the "Forest" whose highest trees came up to our eyeballs. Do you think that is how the forest got its name? By now it was nearly noon, so we didn't expect to find many birds. We were wrong. There was actually a lot of activity, and we got great looks at California Thrashers (lifer, lifer!) As well as California Towhees and Quail. We went back to our room to rest and wait for the 3 o'clock session we had scheduled.

We went over to the library to hear "Meet the Owls." The presenter was a woman who volunteered with a local rehab center. She did a nice job and we got to see a Western Screech-owl, a Barn Owl, and a Great Horned Owl up close and personal. Very neat.

Back to the house for dinner – Perry made spaghetti sauce – and then back to the high school for a presentation by Nigel Marvin. Nigel showed numerous clips from nature films (some that he did with David Attenborough) and told stories and explained how some of the shots were created. Very interesting and entertaining.

We decided to see if we could get on a red-eye flight instead of getting a hotel and leaving late the next

151

morning. Bingo. It cost $100 each to make the switch, but I suspect the hotel might have cost well over $100. In any case, this would get us home about twelve hours earlier than planned. In the morning we joined Perry on his morning coffee expedition and said good-bye to him there.

Then we went over to the Community Center in Morro Bay and met up with the group going out to bird at Montana de Oro. The leader was an old guy who knew where the birds were and had been birding since "he was 13 or so." Bert Something. There were quite a few birds out at the park, and we saw both Wrentit and Bushtit. I was pretty sure the Wrentit was a lifer for both of us [yes, it was]. I think we saw Bushtits in Arizona. I caught a fleeting glimpse of a whale spout off shore, but it wasn't much of a look.

We had lunch at the café next to the Natural History Museum and then walked the wetland trail at the other end of the parking lot. Got a few more birds out there.

At 1:30 we went to hear Louise do her talk about the local heron rookery. She showed some slides she took out there and told us there were some Black-crowned Night-herons just outside the auditorium. So we got one more California bird on the way to our car. We said "good-bye" to Jill and Louise and thanked Louise profusely for inviting us out for the festival. Then we hit the road to LA.

Traffic was horrible, as expected, when we got to the city, and it took nearly two hours for the last ten or fifteen miles. Yuck. We turned in the car at Alamo and caught their shuttle over to the airport. We had a great trip. Good birds. Good people. Mostly good weather. Even without the pelagic trip, we must have gotten nearly 100 California birds. I was too tired to add the last day's sightings to our bird list. I was certain we had seen more than sixty species in any case that day.

Put our California sightings into the database –
we ended up with 101 species for the weekend. Wow. I
got eight lifers, Sue got fifteen – she was only eight
behind me on her ABA list.

# Chapter 20
## West Virginia (one more time) Kentucky and Tennessee
## Monday, May 1 to Friday, May 5, 2006

On Monday we hit the road around 7:40 in the morning and spent most of the day driving to Summersville, West Virginia. We made a brief stop at Cranberry Glades around 4 in the afternoon. It was one of those pockets of habitat left over from the end of the last Ice Age. High in the mountains and very remote. There was a boardwalk built in a loop through the bog and we only ran into two or three other couples on our walk around. We managed to pick up two new West Virginia species - Chipping Sparrow and Blue-headed Vireo - but it was so late in the afternoon there wasn't much of a birdy nature going on. The trail itself was very promising, but we probably wouldn't get back there. One would almost have to camp out at the park to be there at a decent hour in the morning. Either that or leave Summersville at 4 AM to drive back. There were lots of interesting plants in the wetter areas - Pitcher Plants, Marsh Marigolds, and Yellow Birch come to mind. As a kid I was fascinated by carnivorous plants, so the Pitcher Plants were a special treat. Each one grows in the shape of, um, well, a pitcher. Inside this pitcher are hairs pointing downward, so a hapless insect crawling in has little chance of climbing back out. The pitcher also collects rainwater in the bottom which drowns the bugs and provides a transfer medium for the plant's digestive juices. We also spent some time admiring a set of bear tracks that another couple pointed out to us.

We decided to check out Summersville Lake the next morning before continuing on to Kentucky. If the birds didn't show there, we would try a couple of nearby state parks. We still needed seven birds to get to fifty in West Virginia. We were beginning to think the state was not going to give them up.

Tuesday morning we got up around 6 and had breakfast at our motel. Sue had cereal. I had a stale biscuit with tepid sausage gravy and the sort of coffee you suspect was made by waving a brown crayon over a pot of lukewarm water. Yum. The rest of the day was MUCH better. It almost had to be.

We drove down to Summersville Lake and managed to find several new birds. Number 44 turned out to be a Mallard! Don't ask me how we could have visited West Virginia twice before without finding one. A little joke from the Gods of Birding, perhaps. Number 45 was at least a bit more interesting – it was a Broad-winged Hawk. A Ring-billed Gull floated by. Then in rapid succession we found an Eastern Bluebird and a Wood Thrush. Our hopes were starting to soar.

A stop at an overlook near the dam at the end of the lake produced a Tufted Titmouse and an Ovenbird. Numbers 49 and 50 for West Virginia! Hurray for us. State number 35 was completed. Finally.

Getting out of the mountains of West Virginia was pretty slow going so it took longer than we expected to get to Kentucky. When we got to Frankfort, we wanted to check out two nature preserves Sue had found information about. We had an address for one of them - the Clyde E. Buckley Wildlife Sanctuary owned by the Audubon Society. It was off "Germany Street."

Unfortunately, we had no map to locate "Germany Street." So we stopped at an auto body shop and asked for directions. The owner, Mr. M  was a tall sixty-ish balding man with a full beard. Skinny with a Kentucky accent you could cut with a knife. He thought he had an idea about where the place was ("Over near Versailles" – pronounced "Ver-SALES", of course), but his map was probably thirty years old and falling apart at its creases. "I keep meanin' ta git a new one, but I allus fergit." We had the phone number for Audubon on our printout, and damned if he didn't call them and get directions. They were complicated, but I managed to remember enough to get us to where there were signs

155

to lead us the rest of the way in.

It was worth the trouble! We got 22 species there including Indigo Bunting, Wood Thrush and Blue Grosbeak. After we left there we drove all the way down to the exit for Mammoth Cave. We ended up at a Ramada Inn that was not very clean, to be delicate. It was only one night, and we were within walking distance of a Cracker Barrel - where we had dinner.

Curious signs and town names today:

**Lover's Leap Baptist Church**
**Wreck-a-Mended Body Shop**
**Gum Spring Baptist Church**
**Turkey Creek, WV**
**Chimney Corner, WV**
**Alloy, WV**
**Boomer, WV**
**Salt Lick, KY**

Wednesday was a very busy day. It was our ninth anniversary. At least we both remembered. Started out with breakfast at a local Cracker Barrel. Then we birded some around Mammoth Cave National Park before taking the Travertine Tour at 8:45. We counted up our bird list and since we had 51 species for Kentucky, we started driving to Tennessee.

We missed our first exit and decided to take back roads to get back on track. We ultimately made our way to Cross Creeks NWR near Dover, TN. Even though it was mid-afternoon, we found some great birds. As far as we could tell, we already had 51 species for Tennessee, too. We planned to bird strictly for fun the next day and start wending our way back home.

Amusing signs for the day:

**Little Hope Baptist Church**

**Medea's Family Reunion (the mind reels -
kids acting up? Kill the little suckers...)
Golgotha Fun Park (sounds like a blast!)
Sootsus (a chimney sweep service)**

We spent the night at the Hampton Inn in Paris,
TN. After breakfast there we drove over to the Big
Sandy division of the Tennessee National Wildlife
Refuge for a couple of hours of great birding. Highlights
were a Pileated Woodpecker, a Yellow-breasted Chat
and a small covey of Northern Bobwhites.

Next we went up to LBL - the Land Between the
Lakes National Recreation Area, which straddles the
Tennessee/Kentucky border. We found some more
good birds there and saw the resident Bison and Elk
herds - not totally free running, but fun to see anyway.
From there we headed north to hit Interstate 24 and
headed east.

Spent the rest of the day driving. We made a gas
and lunch stop in metropolitan Central City, KY. It was
neither "central" nor a "city" - in fact it was pretty awful.
Lots of signs urging voters to re-elect Mayor Hugh
Sweatt. Wonder if his opponent will make Hugh
Sweatt? Sorry. We ate lunch at a filthy pizza joint.
Enough said. We were tired, and we had our fifty birds
in all three states, so we planned to hit the road early
next morning and go home a couple of days earlier
than planned. We had already covered more than 1500
miles. Yawn.

# Chapter 21
## Iowa-Nebraska-South Dakota completed
## Tuesday, October 3 – Tuesday, October 17, 2006

After flying to Chicago and picking up a rental car, we stopped briefly at Port Louisa NWR in Iowa, where we got 19 species. The refuge was located on the Mississippi River on the southeastern border region of the state. A major portion of the refuge was closed until spring to minimize disturbance to the waterfowl who winter there. That explains why we got so few birds. Of course, it was 93 degrees when we stopped and the birds were smart enough to hunker down in the shade. With the birds we saw along the way, plus a couple of Common Nighthawks seen from the parking lot at our motel in Pella, we had a total of 28 species for Iowa. It was a start.

One reason we stayed in Pella was its proximity to Lake Red Rock, reputed to be a major birding area for the state. We planned to check it out the following morning. The TV in our room had no picture, so the young folks on the staff brought in a second set - couldn't get the broken one unbolted from the dresser. Pretty good security for a place with nothing really worth stealing. All this for a base rate of $59 a night. Breakfast started at 5:30 in the morning, which meant we could get an early start on our quest for the day.

Next morning we drove out to Lake Red Rock, which was on the Des Moines River between Knoxville and Pella. The area provided a variety of ecological niches that included the river valley itself, the lake, marshes, woodlands, and some prairie fragments. We were only able to spend a short time there, so we only managed to find seventeen species, but they included some nice birds - Caspian Terns, White Pelicans, Franklin's Gulls, and a Cooper's Hawk.

We spent most of the rest of the day driving across Iowa to the DeSoto NWR on the western border

158

of the state. It turned out that a big chunk of that refuge is technically in Nebraska! It seems the Army Corps of Engineers changed the course of the Missouri River and Nebraska decided to keep its old border. The good news was that we got a bunch of Iowa AND Nebraska birds. The bad news was that we ended up with just 44 Iowa birds. Nuts. We got some Wilson's Snipe in Iowa and tons of Cedar Waxwings in both states. There was a marker at the DeSoto NWR in the Nebraska section commemorating a place where Lewis and Clark are believed to have camped. Sue took my picture in front of it, since I had actually waded through all of the Lewis and Clark journals.

We decided to eat at the restaurant at our hotel. It was close. We were very tired. It was the easy choice. Our waitress was an attractive young woman who might have been about 20 years old. Attentive, but not annoying.

"Can I get you folks something to drink before dinner?"

"I'd like a glass of Merlot," said Sue.

"Do you have any single malt Scotch?" I queried.

"Um. Single. Ah. Single mulch? Scotch?" she looked puzzled.

"Hmm. Some single malts have a peaty flavor, but aren't really good for mulch as far as I know. How would it be if you took me to the bar and I can see what you have?"

"Good idea. This way."

So we made our way to the dimly-lit bar, and there on the shelf was a full bottle of Glenfiddich. It was dusty. Obviously not much call for such drinks in this part of Nebraska. I pointed to the bottle and said, "That will do just fine. Thank you."

I returned to our table and the waitress soon appeared with a glass of Merlot for Sue and a tumbler of Glenfiddich for me. I am talking about a twelve-ounce water glass with at least eight ounces of Scotch adorning its interior. I was glad we could walk to our

159

room.

As I sipped the Scotch and contemplated the menu, I wondered what such a generous serving was going to cost. In Philadelphia, I would have guessed a minimum of thirty bucks. Dinner was delicious and when the tab appeared, I had to check the drinks. "Scotch: $3.00" it read. If this were a work of fiction, you wouldn't believe that. Maybe you still don't.

Fanfare! Nebraska was done in the quest for 50 birds in 50 states. State number 38. Hurray for us. We got up early and had breakfast at the Holiday Inn where we had stayed. It was not free, but it was a good, hearty breakfast. Then we drove over to Crane Meadows Nature Center. It was closed. Seriously. It wasn't to open until 9 o'clock. That seemed pretty late for a birding hot spot. There were trails, but it wasn't obvious whether we would be welcome to walk them during off hours.

Sooooo, we decided to start out for our next destination - Valentine NWR near, um, Valentine, Nebraska. As we were driving along I-80 we saw a sign for the Lowe Sanctuary and Audubon Center near the town of Lowell. We decided to check it out, since it was still early enough for good birding. The trail led through fields and forested sandhills. We picked up six or seven new birds for Nebraska, including an Eastern Towhee. We also had an encounter with five Wild Turkeys along the road to the Sanctuary. Always a treat.

We spent the rest of the morning driving up to the Valentine NWR, and a couple of hours driving around it. Picked up a ton of birds including TWO lifers - Clay-colored Sparrows and Lapland Longspurs. Drove up to Valentine (the town) and checked into the Comfort Inn. Rested for an hour or so and drove out to Fort Niobrara NWR. First bird we saw there was a Bald Eagle. We drove around the access road that wound through a prairie dog town. They were really cute little buggers. We hiked around the Fort Falls trail and picked up a couple more birds. On our way out we saw three White-tailed Deer and a huge bull Elk. Dinner was at the Peppermill Steakhouse on the corner across from our motel.

We had a great day today. Again! We started out visiting Fort Niobrara NWR in Nebraska. Best bird was a Prairie Falcon. Favorite moment was Sue taking numerous pictures of a huge bull Elk who was very accommodating. Then there was the modest herd of Bison. Plus the expected Prairie Dogs and White-tailed Deer. A nice start for the day. We stopped in beautiful downtown Valentine to fill up the gas tank and get a real breakfast at Mickey D's.

Then we took U.S. Rte. 20 across northern Nebraska to Merriman and turned north to South Dakota. We wended our way to Lacreek NWR near Martin, SD. Drove around the auto route and got some nice birds - Yellow-headed Blackbirds, Trumpeter Swans. Stuff like that. Also watched a Coyote stalking Prairie Dogs until one of them sent out the alarm and foiled his evil plot.

We drove up to Martin and checked in at the Crossroads Inn. Got some lunch at Martin Livestock Auction and Café. I am not making this up. The food was fine, and the folks were friendly. When we headed back to the motel for a wee lie down, there was a huge parade going down the main drag. Well, huge by small-town standards. In a community of 2,000 most of them seemed to be in the parade. Sue took lots of pictures. Most of the signs referred to that night's football game against Pine Ridge. Talk about getting transported all the way back to the 1950s!

We watched some baseball on TV and napped for a while and then went back to Lacreek. We drove a different route and got some new birds for South Dakota - White Pelicans, Belted Kingfisher, Greater Yellowlegs. Did I say new birds for South Dakota? Hell, we got a new bird for life - BURROWING OWLS. Two

161

of 'em. Count 'em. How cool was that. Oh, and there was a young Badger frolicking around the last Prairie Dog town we checked out. He was rolling and jumping and having a good ol' time – it looked like he was chasing grasshoppers. Back at the hotel we watched the Tigers-Yankees playoff game. The umpires as usual were making bad calls in favor of the Yankees. Despite this, the Tigers were leading 3-0 when I fell asleep.

We decided against returning to Lacreek the next morning, and started directly for Hot Springs. Along the way the Gods of Birding deigned to show us a flock of 15-20 Sharp-tailed Grouse. We were zipping along Rte. 18 and Sue spotted something in a tree along the left side of the road. "It was sort of big and shaped like a chicken." Screeeeeech. We made a u-turn and went back to see what was up. There were two grouse in the tree and the rest were feeding in a field right along the road. Wow.

We made a small detour at Wounded Knee and checked out the marker sign for the famous massacre. Near Oglala we spotted a sign urging "Vote for Jackson Ten Fingers." Another suggested we dial 1-800-LOVEGOD."

Eventually we got to Hot Springs and continued on up to Custer State Park. Made a short stop at the Wind Cave National Park visitor center to inquire which roads to Custer State Park were open. Had a nice chat with the woman ranger.

Now that we knew which road to take, we drove up to Custer and over to the state park. Stopped briefly at Sylvan Lake. Drove the Needles Drive. Went all the way around the Wildlife Loop where we saw lots of Pronghorns, some Prairie Dogs and a couple of Bison. Decided to stay in Custer that night and get over to the park early the next morning. Checked in at the Comfort Inn, had a bite to eat at a local steakhouse, watched

Detroit demolish the Yankees in the ALDS. You already know whom we were rooting for.

Next day was a busy one. Started with breakfast at the Comfort Inn in Custer. Then we drove up to Sylvan Lake and walked the trail all the way around it. This involved some entertaining scrambles over the rock formations at the far end. After this circumambulation we drove the Needles Highway again and took the pictures we wished we had taken yesterday. Nothing but beautiful scenery. Then we drove part of the wildlife loop again. Saw lots of Bison, Prairie Dogs and White-tailed Deer. Plus Red Squirrels, Least Chipmunks, Cottontails and five Bighorn Sheep. Among the birds we saw a couple of Harris' Sparrows (lifers), a Golden Eagle, and a flock of about 75 Sandhill Cranes. Other than that it was a pretty routine morning.

Drove down to Hot Springs and checked into the Holiday Inn Express where we would be staying for the Elderhostel. We went downstairs to register for the program and were immediately taken (actually we drove) over to the Mammoth Site for a short orientation. Dinner at the hotel featured a waiter who turned out to be the mayor of Hot Springs. I am not making this up. We appeared to be among the younger participants in the program. The program actually ended on Thursday night, so we would have a bit more breathing room to get our final six Iowa birds.

Monday was our first day of working at the Mammoth Site. The day started with an orientation to the preparation lab by Olga, the director. We were assigned to the group that was supposed to remove sediment deposits from some bones. We spent the morning shift working on small bones - I cleaned up three rib fragments, Sue had a similar group to work on. Then we worked on a skull that was very fragile. I was working on a side portion when a large chunk of sediment broke loose along with some bone fragments. Made me very nervous! We had lunch with the site staff and then worked from 1:30 to 3:30. We had a field trip to a local Nature Conservancy reserve. It would have been a lovely walk except for the rain and the low temperatures. Hmm. We had dinner at the mayor's bowling alley. That guy really got around.

Sue and I spent our second day in the lab. Morning session was devoted to learning about molding and casting replicas of fossils and artifacts. We each got to make a casting to take home. I made the baby mammoth tooth and Sue made the Short-faced Bear claw. At lunch we had a short presentation on the geology of the area.

That afternoon we started by practicing screening techniques. We basically sorted through trays of gravel with various snail shells and rodent bones planted in them. I finished my two trays fairly quickly, and Olga gave me a couple of trays of unchecked sediment to look through. I found lots of bone fragments and the second tray had a number of ivory chips in it. Cathy took us on a tour of the exhibits upstairs to finish the day. We had time to go back to our room and rest before dinner.

Hell, we had time to learn Chinese before dinner as slow as the service was at the restaurant. Some of our party didn't get served until nearly 6:45 - and we were there at 5. We would not be eating there again, evidently. Talk about incompetence. Yikes.

Larry Agenbroad, the local paleontology guru gave an interesting talk about a bison kill site down in Nebraska. I had bought one of his mammoth books at the gift shop that afternoon, so I asked him to autograph it for me. He was very nice. There was, as usual, at least one certifiable character in this group — he called himself "C.L." He was bright and interesting while being annoying in many ways. He only seemed to drink iced tea, and it had to be regular, unsweetened tea. So far he had had little luck procuring any to his liking. He did come out with an amusing quote, though, "That guy talks like a shit salesman with a mouthful of samples."

Our first day of work in the bone bed was rewarding but exhausting. The group total for the previous three days was approaching three tons removed from the site. Wow. I hurt from the neck down.

We had dinner at the Flatiron that night. It was better than Snotty's Steak House. Cathy gave a talk that evening about how broad conclusions can be reached about the data collected at the site. I confess I fell asleep in the middle. I was not the only one. I think Larry Agenbroad will be speaking again tomorrow night for our last official meeting. He promised to tell stories about his research trips to Siberia.

It was around fourteen degrees with a wind chill around three the next morning. Brrrrrrrrrr. At least the wind wasn't blowing too hard. We spent our last day of the Elderhostel digging in the bone bed again. The final total for the group for our four days here was just over four tons of material removed. Not bad for "Old Folks on Safari."

Larry Agenbroad took us for a walk to check out a couple of other sinkholes near the Mammoth Site that afternoon. We had dinner at the Flatiron again. Dr. Agenbroad sat with us, and he was a very easygoing guy. He gave another talk/presentation that evening. This time he (as promised) told us about his work in Siberia. Pretty neat. We had the usual last-night thank yous and evaluations and prizes.

We drove about 500 miles next day from Hot Springs, SD to Estherville, IA.. We managed to see a few species of ducks on a pond along the way in Iowa, so our current list was up to 47 species for the state. We planned to drive to Union Slough NWR next

165

morning to look for our last three Iowa birds. Should we succeed, we would have completed 40 states in our quest for fifty birds in fifty states. Hurray for us! We had dinner at the local bar and grill in Estherville that evening, and the food was reasonable and tasty.

We got our usual early start. Grabbed breakfast at Mickey D's in Estherville and drove over to Union Slough NWR to get our last three birds for Iowa. It was closed. The refuge, not the state. We sat in the parking lot and spotted a Harrier and a Rusty Blackbird, which brought our Iowa total to 49.

We decided to just go on our way and see what we could pick up along the road or at the lakes between us and Wisconsin. We hadn't gone five miles before we spotted a large flock of birds among a herd of Herefords. We stopped, and sure enough some of them were Brown-headed Cowbirds. Yeah. That would be 50 birds in our 40th state. Coooool.

The next several hours were spent driving to Effigy Mounds National Monument on the Mississippi at the eastern end of Iowa. We walked some of the trails and besides the interesting mounds, we managed to find Hermit Thrushes, a Red-headed Woodpecker(!), and a couple or three Bald Eagles. After seeing a couple of Herring Gulls along the way, our final Iowa total that evening came to 54.

We drove past Madison and stopped in Lake Mills because it was where we were and we were pooped. We planned to maybe bird around Milwaukee in the morning and head down to Paula and Rick's in Evanston, IL.

Sign of the day in Wisconsin: **"Mustard Museum – Poupon U."**

The frost was on the pumpkin when we got up next morning. At least it was on our rental car. Brrrrrr. We started out from Lake Mills right after breakfast and

166

drove over to the Schlitz Audubon Center on the north side of Milwaukee. We birded there several years ago when we were visiting Paula and Rick. They had built a huge visitors' center and an observation tower overlooking Lake Michigan since we were last there. Very impressive. So was the birding. Wonderful moment of the morning had to be when we were walking along the beach and a Brown Creeper flew out of the brush and landed on the back of my leg! He proceeding to crawl up my right leg, across my butt and down my left leg. Wow. Of course we didn't have a camera with us, why do you ask? I suspect we will remember it for a long time anyway.

We got twenty-some birds at the center and headed down towards Evanston. Sue was driving, and she decided to take the back roads since we thought Paula and Rick weren't expecting us until late afternoon. We stopped in Racine at a KFC for lunch. Got to the Shaffer's at around 2:45. Visited and ate dinner and started watching the Mets at the Cards. Fell asleep when the score was 2-2.

## Chapter 22
## Hawai'i, Part Two
## Monday, January 29 – Wednesday, February 7, 2007

Monday morning we got up around 4 and were on the road by 5, maybe a little before. Arrived at the airport by 6:30 and were through security by 7:30. Our flight was scheduled to leave at 8:25, so we were in great shape. Of course, Northwest didn't even bring our plane out until departure time. By the time we boarded the plane and stopped to have the wings de-iced we were a good hour late getting off the ground. Somehow we managed to just catch our connecting flight in Minneapolis by sprinting between gates with our carry-on luggage. It was a good aerobic workout for the middle of a day that was mostly devoted to sitting in cramped airplane seats.

We got to Honolulu in plenty of time to catch the puddle jumper to Lihu'e on the island of Kaua'i. No, of course our luggage wasn't on that flight. It didn't race between gates in Minneapolis the way we did. So I filled out a claim form and assumed we might see our luggage sometime later in the week.

The cab ride from Lihu'e Airport to the Aloha Beach Resort in Kapa'a took a matter of minutes. It was a lovely hotel. Being pretty much spent from our long flights, we had room service bring us dinner. We had just finished eating when guess what? Our luggage arrived looking a bit sheepish about having that extra drink to ward off the cold in Minnesota. So we had clean clothes and were totally exhausted. We went right to bed. I fell asleep wondering how many places we had been that had glottal stops in their names. Lihu'e...Kaua'i...Kapa'a...

The weather was what the Brits would call "dodgy" off and on our first full day on Kaua'i. We had breakfast at the hotel at 6:30 and then went for a birding walk along the beach. We managed to find eighteen species and some of them were pretty nice - the pair of Great Frigatebirds comes to mind, a couple of White-rumped Shamas, some Pacific Golden Plovers, and two different Mannikins (Nutmeg and Chestnut (a.k.a. Black-headed Munias). In the course of the day we added three species to our Hawai'i list. Seventeen to go.

While walking along the beach, which we had pretty much to ourselves, we saw four or five Humpbacked Whales just off the coast. One of them even showed us its flukes as it dived. Or possibly as it dove. Definitely NOT duve.

We walked over to "town" around noon and picked up some snack foods and soft drinks. Sue stayed in the room this afternoon. She was tired for some reason. I went for a walk down along the shore again and took some pictures. Most of them stank, so I deleted them, but a few were at least decent. Took some artsy-fartsy shots of rocks and driftwood and a couple of them weren't terrible. I was struck by the solitude the beach offered – nothing like the throngs on Oahu. Nor the thongs, for that matter.

We registered with the Elderhostel group at five and had dinner with them. The main birding guide, Dan Lindsay, gave a little talk about Hawai'ian birds. The group seemed pretty pleasant and bright, so it looked like we should have a great week.

Wednesday was our first full day of birding with the group. We really liked the leaders – Dan Lindsay, Les C and Dale R. (I have Dan's permission to use his full name...) We were traveling in three vans, and the group was a bit too large. Evidently an earlier trip had not made up, so they doubled us up. By our reckoning, twelve to fifteen is a reasonable maximum for a birding group. There were more than twenty of us this time. Nearly half were not birders at all.

In any case we visited a couple of National Wildlife Refuges - Hanalei, Kilauea Lighthouse Point and Huleia. Um, that was one more than a couple, I suppose. It was very windy most of the day except at the lighthouse, where the wind might have encouraged more seabird activity.

"I'm not going home until I see a Nene," I announced to Dan.

"Well, it is just after 8 o'clock, and you can probably head home in about a half hour, then."

Dan grinned as he said this. He expected we would be seeing at least one small flock of the state bird of Hawai'i at our first stop. Of course he was right. He was the local bird guru. So I switched my quest bird smoothly to the I'iwi – the iconic red endemic honeycreeper with the sickle-shaped bill that always seems to show up on the cover of books with names like *Birds of Hawai'i* and such. Dan said that one would not be seen until a few more days into the trip and I was relieved to learn that I had a justification for staying on.

In spite of the wind (and lack of it when we needed some) we saw a number of wonderful birds, including two that I had personally lusted after - Nene and Laysan Albatross. To be honest, I didn't realize the Laysan Albatross was even found in Hawai'i. For some reason, I thought I would have to go to Midway or some similar remote location to see one.

Another good bird we found during the day was the Japanese Bush-Warbler. Jim G (a fellow participant) teamed up with me to track one down, and we both got great looks at it. Our state total was up to thirty-eight, so we were getting more and more optimistic about making our fifty. I was also pretty certain that we had at least 100 species for the month of January. But that is the story of another quest.

We spotted another couple of Humpback Whales off the point by the Kilauea Lighthouse. There was a fellow on the trip (David S) that reminded us so much of my old department chairman that it was almost creepy. Same face. Same posture. Same mannerisms.

170

There were some serious birders as well as some annoying gits in the group. One of the women on the trip seemed bright enough, but droned on and on with a monotone commentary on the bleeding obvious. It was grating after a while. Fortunately, my brain has had the good taste to erase her name from my memory banks.

Of course Drone had nothing on the poor old soul who was losing her mental faculties. To protect the innocent, we'll call her Dementia. Every morning when she saw a Mynah, she would exclaim, "That's a very pretty bird! What is that?" And Dan would patiently explain that it was called a Mynah. This happened, sadly, a number of times every day. She also had trouble with taking turns. Evidently she had regressed to the pre-kindergarten stage. The protocol was that we would rotate our seats regularly in the vans so everyone had a chance to sit up front and no one was stuck all the way in the back all of the time. As a general rule, we switched about every twenty to thirty minutes. When it came time for Dementia to relinquish the front seat, she assured everyone that she had only been there for "two or three minutes." Fortunately, the rest of the group was very kind and tolerant. Not much choice, when you think about it. We were all too painfully aware that we could be in the same place in a few years.

The weather on Thursday wasn't dodgy. It was horrible. We drove up into the mountains to look for forest birds - especially endemics. It rained so hard we were soaked through to the skin as soon as we stepped out of the vans. The good news is we actually got good looks at Apapane - Sue had not seen them when we birded on Oahu two years earlier and I had only caught a fleeting glimpse. The Apapane was a tiny red bird that seemed to like to hang out up high in trees. The sort of elevations that give birders what is affectionately known as "Warbler Neck."

We spotted one feral pig and I caught a glimpse

of a flock of wild goats up by Waiamea Canyon. The canyon itself was totally invisible in the fog. Well, 99% invisible anyway. I did see that feral pig.

The weather cleared up somewhat by lunchtime and we birded a couple of wetland sites. Sue (and several others not including her husband) saw a Short-eared Owl. Other exciting birds included a Snow Goose and a pair of Tundra Swans - both quite rare in Hawai'i, according to Dan. My favorite life bird for the day was the Wandering Tattler. Is that a great bird name or what? Why tattler? Whom is it squealing on? Damned if I know. Our state list was at 46 at the end of our third day, so we figured we had a good chance to get over fifty species before we left the following Tuesday.

Friday was a travel day - we flew first from Lihu'e on Kaua'i to Honolulu. Then from Honolulu to Hilo on the Big Island. Dementia had another of her crises of understanding when she asked where we were. "Hawai'i," someone assured her. "I know we're in Hawai'i. What island?" "Hawai'i – the big island is CALLED Hawai'i." "But where are we?" You get the idea. Poor old soul.

We got there around 11:30 AM and had a picnic lunch in a local state park. Then we looked for birds in the park and got enough new ones to push our state total over the magic 50 mark! Hurray for us! Again.

You could never guess what our fiftieth bird was for Hawai'i, so I'll tell you right now: Northern Shoveler! Seriously. There were a number of birds on the ponds in the state park that are common on the mainland. Our birds 47-50 were: Greater White-fronted Goose, American Wigeon, Northern Pintail and the aforementioned Shoveler. Hey, they were new for us in Hawaii!

As we were driving around that afternoon a Mongoose ran across the road, so that was new for our mammal list for the year. We also stopped at a park along the coast and watched a Green Sea-turtle

172

grazing on algae. Of course I took a picture and missed the time he stuck his head up to get a breath. Rats. I did get a nice picture of a spot in the water where a turtle was just a second ago.

My throat had been sore since the plane ride from Minneapolis on Monday and it finally blossomed into laryngitis. Poopingness.

We were staying in a fancy schmancy hotel that charged extra for internet access. It wasn't all that expensive, but I decided I didn't need it that badly. I am not mentioning the hotel name, because they don't deserve a free plug. Besides, I can't remember it anyway. "That's a pretty bird..."

The group spent about an hour Saturday morning exploring the Farmers Market (no apostrophe on purpose) in Hilo before heading out for some serious birding and sight-seeing. Sue found some Hawai'ian clothes for the grandkids as well as a native flute for herself. Skipping the shopping, I found two Yellow-billed Cardinals in the parking lot who were flitting from car to car and arguing with their reflections in the rearview mirrors. What a hoot!

At Hawai'i Volcanoes National Park we started our visit by walking through the Nahuku Lava Tube. It was essentially a natural tunnel formed, I suppose, by gases escaping through the lava before it solidified into rock.

In the forest were good numbers of Apapane as well as a few thrushes called 'Oma'o. There are two glottal stops in that one – I have no idea how to BEGIN a word with a glottal stop. The Hawai'ians do it all the time, though. It is just another consonant to them.

The group drove the Chain of Craters Road over to the Holei Sea Arch. The purpose of our stop there was to see Black Noddies around the arch, but no one had told them and they were still off somewhere, presumably drinking Kona coffee. The scenery was still stunning.

173

As we were walking that morning, Dan asked whether any of us had taken geology in college. He maintained that it was one of the easiest courses at the University of Hawaii. The class went out on a field trip the first day. The professor pointed to pretty much any rock and said, "That is basalt. The final exam will be tomorrow."

We stopped at Halema'uma'u Crater which was full of steaming fumaroles. Isn't that a great word: "fumarole." Sounded like a creative insult as in "Leave me alone you stupid fumarole!" Hmm. I might be able to use that some day. In reality, they were simply breaks in the rock that allowed smoke and steam to escape from the hot lava below.

We had a late lunch at the head of the trail at Kipuka Puaulu Special Ecological Area, a.k.a. the "Bird Park." The predominant species was again Apapane, although we saw good numbers of Kalij Pheasants as well. They were pretty cool, even if they were an introduced species. We made a brief stop at the visitors' center on the way back and we managed to find a souvenir patch at the Volcano House Hotel gift shop. It was a good day, but we were very tired.

My cold seemed a bit better, but I was still voiceless like many Japanese vowels. Now THAT is an obscure reference. I'm afraid I need to explain that one for my readers who have not studied Japanese. There are many vowels in Japanese that are simply elided over, hence the term "voiceless." A good example occurs in the common woman's name, Yoshiko. Most of us Anglophones would pronounce that something like "yo-SHEE-ko. In actual Japanese pronunciation, it comes out "YOSH-ko. No middle vowel at all. In any case, it wasn't just my vowels that were voiceless, I could barely squeak.

The next day we were scheduled to go after a number of Hawai'ian endemics. I didn't care how tired I was or how sick! I vowed to get those birds. There was a fellow giving a talk on the endemic birds the evening I

174

wrote this, but I couldn't see myself staying awake to hear it. Especially since he seemed unable to get his projector and computer to talk to each other. Maybe they had had a fight. We didn't stay around to see the outcome.

Most of Sunday was spent driving out to Hakalau Forest National Wildlife Refuge. The last ten miles were on one of the roughest roads we had ever seen – it reminded us of the road across the Chiricahuas in Arizona. You know, where the smoothest parts were the cattle barriers. Actually there were very short paved bits every so often where they were trying to prevent total washouts, I guess. It was mildly humorous after, say, thirty yards of paved road to find a sign announcing "Pavement Ends". Gee, we couldn't see fifteen feet in front of us. Thanks for the warning.

In any case, we had access to part of the refuge that was not generally open to the public. We got several endemic species, including 'I'iwi, Elepaio, Nene, Hawai'ian Creeper. Sue walked farther than I felt up to and got an Akepa and an 'I'o. So much for my vow to keep going no matter what. I couldn't do it.

The weather was beautiful. We had dinner at the Coconut Grille. It was mediocre. We were enjoying several of our companions while others, of course, were totally annoying. Just like real life. Oh, and I still had no voice.

Monday morning we drove up the Saddle Road to Pu'ula'au in search of a Palila. Say that three times quickly. We managed to get everyone good looks at one by about 10:30, so the rest of the day was spent stopping at various "hot spots" looking for miscellaneous introduced species. We also were told we could claim to have driven the entire Saddle Road, for what that was worth. Maybe a footnote in the Guinness Book of World Records? Probably more like a footnote to a footnote.[11]

The birdiest stop was at the Makalei Hawai'i Country Club where we got great looks at African Silverbills (now called White-faced Munias), Saffron Finches and a Red Avadavat. Does that last one sound like some sort of legal deposition to you? Sue saw a Yellow-fronted Canary, but most of the group [again including her husband] never found it. Alas. The two pains-in-the-arse of the group convinced us that we would be glad to go home soon. Our favorite couple in the group had to be Jim and Jan G, two retired physicians who lived in California. On the whole it was a good trip. We got a nice group of Hawai'ian endemics as well as lots of introduced birds that were lifers for us. Aloha.

Our plane didn't leave on Tuesday until 4 in the afternoon, so we had time for a birding walk around the Japanese garden near the hotel that morning. We got fifteen species of birds, a mongoose and a green sea-turtle. We checked out of the hotel around 11:30 and shared a cab to the airport with Bill and Barb K from the Elderhostel group.

Sue asked at the gate whether there was room on an earlier flight to Honolulu and we ended up leaving at 1:30 instead of 4 something. That meant we got to sit around the Honolulu airport for three or four hours instead of Hilo. Honolulu was bigger and there were more food choices, plus I managed to locate a Red-vented Bulbul while waiting. Well, actually, he located me and sat on a sign above my chair briefly. Our Northwest flight from Honolulu to Minneapolis was delayed, of course. The flight from Minneapolis to Philly was NOT, and we barely caught it. This felt familiar for some reason. We got to the gate as they were starting general boarding. Our assumption was that our luggage would be making its way home separately. Again.

---

[11] Sorry. I couldn't stop myself...

Wednesday we got back home and I'll be damned. Our luggage was among the first to appear on the carousel in Philly that morning. It was a miracle! The temperature drop from Honolulu to Philadelphia was only about 60 degrees Fahrenheit. At least the roads were clear. We stepped into our house at just about noon and spent the afternoon sorting through mail, updating bird sightings, doing laundry, calling Mom, and the usual post-travel stuff.

Our final Hawai'i bird totals: Jim 71, Sue 74. I got twenty lifers and Sue presumably got 23. A very productive trip. Fun, too! My cold was much better, although I still sounded like a bereft bullfrog.

# Chapter 23
## North Dakota and Montana (completed)
## Wednesday, June 13 – Wednesday, June 20, 2007

Ah, Fargo, North Dakota. A town whose very name evokes visions of long, freezing winters and the isolation of the open plains. Of course the real town is pretty much like any other small city in America. Strip malls. The same chain stores you would see in Pennsylvania or Georgia or New Mexico. Of course, you don't see as many grain elevators on the east coast or in the high desert.

The weather in Fargo was awful when we arrived Wednesday afternoon. Raining. Raining. Raining as in a cloudburst. We picked up our rental car from Enterprise and headed west. As we covered the eighty miles from Fargo to Jamestown the weather got better and better. By the time we had dinner, the sun was shining. Our "On the Road" list for North Dakota already boasted about a dozen species. The next day we would start the quest in earnest.

Thursday morning came with a heavy fog that obscured everything and we were afraid we might not be able to do much birding. As we drove north the fog thinned out and was pretty much gone by the time we reached Arrowwood NWR near the town of Edmunds.

As we suspected might happen, we had our fifty birds for North Dakota by about ten o'clock. There were tons of White Pelicans at the refuge. We saw a half dozen or so Black Terns. Lots of Clay-colored Sparrows. A handful of Bohemian Waxwings (lifer, lifer). Plus we broke our streak of not having seen a Belted Kingfisher for several months. White-tailed Deer, several dozen Bison, and a few Cottontail Rabbits joined our North Dakota mammal list. Plus Sue saw a Muskrat.

A male Northern Harrier flew into sight. With his loops and swoops and dips and dives he could have

gotten a job barnstorming back in the day. He was trying his best to impress the girls with his fitness for breeding. It's how you get chicks in their culture.

Western Grebes are black and white waterfowl about the size of large ducks. With swan-like curving necks and sharply-pointed beaks there is a suggestion of royalty in the way they carry their heads. Could be snobbishness. When we spotted a couple of pairs on the pond, we were pleased to see these old friends. As we watched, two of them started flapping their wings and slapping the water with their feet as if about to take off. Instead of flying, they simply propelled themselves ten or twenty yards and then settled back into the water. It was a courtship display affectionately known as "walking on water." It inspired us to grab our cameras out of the car and inspired the grebes to stop displaying. You don't want someone taking pictures of your sex life, do you? No comment if you do.

Along the way to Fort Totten we saw a large propane tank with the legend "Sioux-per Propane." Groan. I love terrible puns. The badder the better. The drive took less time than we expected, and we got to the Inn by about one.

The Totten Trail Historic Inn was a restored portion of the Fort Totten community from the late nineteenth century. Actually it was a B&B version of the old officers' quarters for, um, Fort Totten. The rooms boasted period furniture - we had a four-poster bed, for example, with step stools on either side for literally climbing into bed. Otherwise, one would have had to pole vault to get up that high.

The entire place was stuffed with antiques and charm. Each room was furnished by a presumably well-to-do local family. A notice on the back of the door informed guests that all of the antiques had been inventoried. If any were missing after a guest's stay, it would be assumed they wanted to purchase the item and it would be charged to their credit card. I suppose that was nicer than warning of criminal penalties for thievery.

The proprietor of the inn, Marlene, was very nice. She recommended we have dinner at Kneadful Things in Devil's Lake - which was owned and operated by a good friend of hers. It was a bakery as well as a restaurant. A nice light supper there - we both had salads – was given special charm by a long chat with the co-owner, Liz J, who was a former figure-skating teacher! Her husband, Dan, was the chef.

Liz was fighting a personal crusade to raise the food consciousness of her corner of North Dakota. She explained to local customers that her breads were not loaded with preservatives, so of course they got stale after a day or two. She told us about her discussion with a food distributor during which she exclaimed in exasperation, "I don't want products, I want ingredients!"

On the way back to Fort Totten we stopped at the Four Winds Casino The casino is one of those modern places run by Native Americans on their own land. Sue won about eighty bucks playing electronic poker, so I talked her into leaving rather than pissing it away. We did drive over to Sully's Hill and had a look around. Despite having signed up online for several events, we were not, in fact, registered for anything there, so we signed up for the stuff we thought we might want to attend. Then we walked one of the trails and saw a few birds. It was mid-afternoon, so not much was about.

Friday was the first day of the actual birding festival at Sully's Hill. We got up around five and had breakfast around ten of six so we could get to the bird walk by 6:30. Fortunately, the fellow who was going to lead the walk was staying at the Inn, so we knew they would not be starting without us. Well, at least not without the leader.

The walk was excellent in terms of the variety of birds. There were 'way too many people on the walk -

at least thirty, I'm guessing. As the group spread out further and further along the trail we were seldom anywhere near the leader. Fortunately, there were a number of us who were experienced birders sprinkled through the crowd and we spotted birds on our own. At the end we had a list that was only a couple of species shy of the group total.

After the walk Sue and I went back to the hotel for a wee lie down. We returned to Sully's Hill for lunch with the group. The food was cheap and basic, but OK. At least they gave us a choice of raw veggies instead of chips and such. We attended two talks – one on shore birds and the other on prairie sparrows. They were both good.

We decided not to hang around for the talk on the people and birds of Iceland. The chairs weren't that comfortable and the topic seemed to lack immediacy.

We drove up to Devil's Lake to see when Mickey D's opened in the morning. It had a 24-hour drive-thru, so we assumed we should be able to get breakfast the next morning. The plan was to meet at 6 up there to take the bus to Alice Lake. Or possibly Lake Alice.

We spent some time that afternoon driving around Sully's Hill again. Checked out the prairie dog town and got some pictures of babies. Also took pictures of bison. That evening there were presentations by two Native Americans. Keith Bear was a flute-playing storyteller, and he was very good. Monica Mayer was a Mandan-Hidatsu-Arikara physician who gave a disorganized presentation on the medical side of the Lewis and Clark Expedition. Potentially interesting, at least, but totally impossible to follow in execution. This may have been when I learned the trivia item that Lewis and Clark's latrines are still detectable because of the mercury compounds they used for medicinal purposes.

The next morning we got up at five so we could meet the Lake Alice group at six in Devil's Lake. We bought breakfast at McDonald's as planned and met the group in the parking lot at Walmart. Was this an All-American trip or what? They took us up to Lake Alice NWR in an old school bus. It appeared to be the same vintage as the ones I rode to school in the 1950s. Boy, did that bring back memories. Some pleasant, some not so much. It wasn't a very long ride, thank goodness. The nostalgia wore off in about two minutes.

At the refuge we walked about a mile around one of the roads. We were very glad we didn't chicken out because of the warning to wear boots. The road was perfectly dry and our sneakers were just fine.

Speaking of fine, the birding was more than that. Highlights included finding a Killdeer nest with four eggs in it - we knew it was close because Mama was doing her best injured bird act - "Look at me over here! My wing is broken! Pay no attention to those eggs on the ground! Please!" We also saw a baby Avocet. Our fearless leader, Mark, described it as a Q-tip – long legs with a blob of fuzz on top. Cute as hell, though. I also got a look at a baby Coot. The fellow I was walking with at the moment found it with his scope and asked if I knew what it was. The adults are black with prominent white beaks. The babies are small balls of red fluff. Go figure.

Mark also pointed out a couple of flocks of drake Mallards who were flying into the heavy cattails in preparation for their annual flight-feather molt. Since they cannot fly for several weeks, they need to hide out someplace. Mark called it a "molt migration." Never heard that term before.

By the time we finished and went back to Devil's Lake our North Dakota list was up to 95 birds. Sue and I were so tired when we got back to Fort Totten that we went over to the Inn for a nap. I woke up first and cranked up the computer and discovered that the internet connection was finally working.

Anyway, we drove up to Devil's Lake and had lunch at Kneadful Things again. Also bought some more of Liz's cookies to take on our drive the next day. We stopped at the gift shop at Sully's Hill and got presents for our grandchildren.

Late in the afternoon we went over to Sully's Hill and they were getting a nice crowd for the fiddler concert. We got veggie packs for supper and then drove around the auto routes. When we finished, it was only 7:20 and we decided to skip the evening bird walk. We did see the Bison again as well as Prairie Dogs and a young bull Elk. We planned to get an early start in the morning.

We had breakfast at Ft. Totten at six. Marlene fixed me a couple of scrambled eggs and we had cinnamon buns, too. We were on the road by about 6:45 and drove through intermittent rain all morning. The speed limit was 70 most of the way, and we got to Williston around eleven.

We stopped at the Generic Motel and reserved a room for the night. Topped up the gas tank. Got some sandwiches at the local Subway and headed on over to Montana to get our last twenty-five birds there. Along the way, we passed our second billboard of the day with the motto: *Gentlemen, Start Your Augers.* (Sue took a photo of it on the way back.) We knew we were in serious farm country!

The weather stayed heavily overcast and occasionally drizzly the rest of the day. Our target was the Medicine Lake NWR a bit off Route 16 north of Froid. The birding at the refuge was pretty much spectacular all afternoon. Gray Partridge. Lark Buntings. Marbled Godwits. Upland Sandpipers. Baird's Sparrows (lifer!). White Pelicans by the dozen. Wilson's Phalarope. About a zillion Eared Grebes. An American Bittern. A couple of Avocets. You get the idea.

We took the auto tour route which was great until we missed a turn on the back nine and ended up crunching along a pair of tractor tracks that looked like they led off to infinity. The good news was that we got some of our best birds back there. The bad news is we got completely lost. We eventually hit a dirt road (a decided improvement over the tractor ruts) and it occurred to me to crank up my GPS receiver to get a compass bearing. We were, of course, headed in the wrong direction. Hey, it was overcast, so we couldn't navigate by the sun. Not that my sense of direction is worth much even when the sun is out.

We finally stopped at a sort of farm house. The house was a nondescript rancher with asbestos shingle siding facing a small barn. A clean pickup truck in the yard complemented a filthy sedan in the garage. There was a squashed rat in the driveway. Two dogs came out to greet us - one looked like a Corgi and one was a mutt named "Utah." Eventually a middle-aged generic blonde woman with stringy hair came out and gave us directions. She also taught us to pronounce Froid correctly. It sounds like the famous Austrian father of psychiatry rather than the French word for "cold."

In the actual town of Froid, which we had to pass through on our way back to North Dakota, there was a ball field named Fjeseth Field. We did not learn how to pronounce that one correctly or otherwise. Obviously we made it back to Williston, but we were a bit nervous for a while there. Well, Sue was more nervous than I was. She was driving...

Back in Williston and had an early supper at the local Applebee's. Checked into the Generic Motel. We saw a half dozen or so White-tailed Deer, several Richardson's (I think) Ground Squirrels, and three or four 13-striped Ground Squirrels. Oh and a handful of Monarch and Cabbage White butterflies.

We slept in (well by our standards) until nearly seven the following morning. Had a big breakfast at the Generic Hotel (whose real name turned out to be El Rancho.) Drove over to the north section of Theodore Roosevelt National Park with a stop in Wafton to get some gas. It was very windy all day. I was severely buffeted at the gas pump. And I don't mean served a selection of foods at a big table.

We got to the park around 8:30. The visitor's center didn't open until 9. We decided to drive part of the scenic route and it was worth our trouble. We stopped to check out a couple of birds along the way and one was a Lazuli Bunting and the other was a Mountain Bluebird. Both new for our North Dakota list and the trip. The scenery was a mixture of badlands and scattered trees.

We stopped at the visitor's center on our way out and found a patch for our banner as well as a copy of Teddy Roosevelt's autobiography and a memory card game for our granddaughter, Syd. Then we went to the southern section of the park and drove around for a couple of hours. More beautiful scenery.

We made a brief visit to Medora around lunch time. Didn't feel much like lunch, so we just got a couple of bottles of pop (notice the local dialect.) Sue bought us each a hoodie at the general store because the wind was cold. We browsed the bookstore (and I didn't buy anything!)

After Medora we headed east and decided to check out part of the Enchanted Highway. There had been an article in the last Smithsonian magazine about the sculptor who had built the world's largest metal structures along the road in an attempt to save the town of Regent from economic ruin. We checked out three of the six completed sculptures - *Geese in Flight, Deer Crossing,* and *Grasshoppers in the Field.* Unfortunately, most of the *Deer Crossing* installation had collapsed, probably from the wind. Did I mention the wind? It was blowing steadily between twenty and forty miles per hour all day. The famous prairie wind that drove some pioneers to madness. It was supposed to lessen by midnight. Or after midnight. Before we were driven to madness, I hoped.

After the giant grasshopper sculpture we decided to head for Bismarck. The Comfort Inn gave us vouchers for two free drinks, and it turned out they had free appetizers in the lounge. Sue had a glass of Merlot and I had a Jameson's. The appetizers served as dinner.

Plus in the south section of the national park we saw a dozen or so Bison, hundreds of Prairie Dogs, and about 10 wild horses. In the north section we saw a couple of White-tailed Deer and a Cottontail. Along the Enchanted Highway south of Lefor we saw a Red Fox.

The Comfort Inn in Bismarck served a very generous breakfast in the morning. Scrambled eggs (powdered, of course), sausage links, toast, juice. Good deal.

We hit the road a little after seven and headed for Chase Lake NWR north of Medina, ND. There was a sign in Medina for a Chase Lake information center down a side street, and luckily we checked it out. It was dark inside, but the door was open and I managed to find a bird list and a map of some of the best birding spots in the area. Good thing, or we would have been totally lost most of the day. We found some nice birds, including several new ones for North Dakota and the trip. We had well over one hundred birds on both counts. 108 for North Dakota, to be exact. How cool was that? We got a Swainson's Hawk and Grasshopper Sparrows among others. We also heard some Baird's Sparrows (now that we knew their song.) Along the way we saw a lot of Killdeer doing their broken-wing act. We looked for nests but never found any. We managed to find three baby Killdeer and they were cute as buttons. Well, more like Q-tips. At one point we came across a Moose! That was completely unexpected, although the habitat was perfect for one. Among the other critters spotted were a large Red-bellied Turtle, a White-tailed Deer, and several butterflies - Monarchs, Red Admirals and Cabbage Whites. There were some large black butterflies, but I never got a good look at any of them. The wind was

186

much less intense and the sun was shining. It was a beautiful day to be alive!

We got to Fargo about two o'clock and checked at the airport to see whether we could get a flight home that day. No luck, but we did find a flight that left early in the morning and got to Philly three hours earlier than our original itinerary. And the change only cost fifty bucks. We walked across to Applebee's for dinner. We split an appetizer sampler. I had a Sam Adams. Sue had a Perfect Margarita. The Germans wore gray, you wore blue.

We got up at 4:30 and had a light breakfast at the motel before heading for the airport. I dropped Sue off near the check-in area and took the car back to the lot. Dropped off the key at the Enterprise desk (and they emailed me the receipt that afternoon.) Met up with Sue at the Northwest desk. When she tried to check herself in she got a message that our "special fares" meant it would cost $200 PER PERSON to change to the earlier flight instead of the $25 per person she paid yesterday. We went to a real person and she checked us in without incident and *without* further payments.

Miracle of miracles, both flights left about when they were scheduled and we landed in Philly around 2:30. This meant we were home by the time we would have been starting out from Minneapolis. Well, maybe not quite, but it was a lot nicer driving home at three than it would have been at five-thirty.

# Chapter 24
## Oregon and Washington
### Tuesday, September 4 – Wednesday, September 19, 2007

Some trips turn out OK despite inauspicious beginnings. For our assault on the birds of Oregon and Washington, we got up around 2:30 a.m. Hit the road by 3:30. Arrived at the Northwest Airlines ticket counter in the Philadelphia Airport by about 4:30. Unfortunately, our reservations were with <u>Delta</u>. The Expedia itinerary was not clear about that. The good news is the Delta counter was right next door. The bad news is there was a long line and inadequate staff to check folks in. Aargh. In any case, our flight left at about 6:30 as scheduled and we got to Cincinnati in plenty of time to catch our connection to Portland.

We stopped at the Smith and Bybee Wetlands Natural Area. It was described as an "urban freshwater wetland." There were about two thousand acres tucked in the middle of a sprawling blight of warehouses and factories – sorry, an "industrial area" – Smith and Bybee was meant to absorb flood waters near the point where the Willamette River meets the Columbia. We hiked through part of the shrub swamp whose plant community was dominated by willow thickets and, um, small shrubs.

It was the wrong time of day. The sky was overcast. We didn't get too many birds there, so we drove up to Astoria where we had a nice greasy lunch at the KFC right at the west end of Route 30. Since we don't live far from the east end, the highway reminded us of home. Sort of. We had no plans to drive the entire length and experience the middle bits. 30 links up with 101 there, and we continued on to Fort Clatsop for my Lewis and Clark fix.

For those of you who are not Lewis and Clark junkies, Fort Clatsop is where the Corps of Discovery spent the winter of 1805-1806 once they reached the west coast. The park service had built replicas of the original buildings, including a curious feature I didn't recall reading about. They made their chimneys out of wood. Granted, it was sort of a sort of openwork design, but it still seemed odd to build any sort of chimney out of wood. You will not be shocked to learn that a couple of years before our visit, the barracks burned to the ground. Can you guess why?

We got some nice birds near the fort (Common Merganser, Steller's Jay, Common Yellowthroat, Northern Flicker) and headed down Route 101. Along the way we stopped a couple of times and saw dozens of Brown Pelicans, lots of Western Gulls, and about thirty Harbor Seals. We ended the day with a 22-species start on our Oregon list. Spent the night in Garibaldi.

We had a very busy and birdy day working our way down the coast from Garibaldi to Newport. Our Oregon list was up to 38 species according to Mr. Computer at the end of the day. We drove quite a bit of the Three Capes Loop and made a productive stop at Cape Meares. We got White-winged and Surf Scoters there as well as a Chestnut-backed Chickadee. We also paid a brief visit to the Octopus Tree and Sue got a nice picture of the lighthouse.

Our next stop was at the Whalen Island Clay Myers Natural Area. We hiked the loop trail of about a mile and a half. The trail threaded its way through both fresh- and salt-water wetlands, a bit of grassland and a mixed forest fragment. Got our best birds within the first hundred yards – a Wilson's Warbler and a Chestnut-backed Chickadee. We did get a good look at a Red-shouldered Hawk and a Belted Kingfisher on the back nine, but the hike was starting to remind us of some of our Bataan Death March re-enactments.[12] Except, of course, it was much cooler.

We stopped for lunch in Pacific City at the Pelican Pub and Brewery. Good food. Good local beer made on the premises. The cream ale was delicious. Sue drove all the way and I slept most of the way down to Newport. As I said, the cream ale was delicious.

Once we got to Newport, we made our way over to the "historic bay area" for a look-see and had a light dinner at the Rogue Ales Public House. After we ate, we checked out the sea lions that were hauled out on the rocks and piers in the bay. Very entertaining. Very LOUD. Did I mention smelly? Sue took some good pictures. We were pretty tired that night, having walked over 11,000 steps in the course of the day.

We got up around six the next morning, and Sue couldn't find her shower cap, so she used the ice bucket liner from our room. Quite a fashion statement! For some reason, the computer would not connect to the internet. Of course, I had planned to send our postcards online. Harumph. I re-booted the damned thing, and it worked fine. So I sent postcards to friends and family via Amazing Mail.

After breakfast we birded our way around Yaquina Bay with a brief stop at Yaquina Lighthouse first. We got some good birds – there were three or four Pigeon Guillemots near the lighthouse – lifer! Lifer! Plus we figured out that some of the gulls were Glaucous-winged, another life bird. Oregon was definitely living up to its reputation for beautiful scenery. Wow.

We birded our way down as far as Coos Bay that afternoon. Looked around a bit at Waldport. Not many interesting birds, but saw a ground squirrel. Stopped for

---

[12] There is a county park near us where we usually get lost and refer to our attempts to find our car as such a re-enactment. Usually the temperatures are in the nineties when we visit.

lunch at a little diner just south of Florence. A real slice of Americana.

For dinner we drove down to Charleston and ate at the Portside Restaurant. We had a very nice meal. Sue had prime rib and I had China fish – a local and seasonal bottom fish. My fish was served with toasted almond slices and Dungeness crab meat. Delicious.

A good portion of the next morning was spent driving from Coos Bay to Klamath Falls. A lot of beautiful scenery along the way. A little way north of Diamond Lake we had to wait for a construction delay. We were at the front of the line, and the flagperson (how p.c. is that?) chatted with us. He told us about a couple whose camper caught fire during the winter and they couldn't believe there was no fire department to call. He said he should have called the local "redneck fire department" and had them grab their shovels to throw snow on the fire. What a character.

We made a brief stop at Diamond Lake in order to have a moseying contest – it lasted about five seconds. Sue said she won. She always says she won. My moseying ability evidently needed work. We did get our fiftieth Oregon bird there – I thought  it was the Red-breasted Nuthatch, but it was actually the Northern Shoveler. The nuthatch was number 59. I told you I couldn't count. We also were treated to great looks at a Brown Creeper.

Next on the agenda was a stop at Crater Lake. We took some beautiful pictures and picked up a couple of new birds – the Clark's Nutcrackers were my favorites. Also got a life mammal – Golden Mantled Ground Squirrel and a life butterfly – California Tortoiseshell.

From there we headed down to Klamath Falls with a stop along Upper Klamath Lake. At the lake we got a bunch of great birds – Long-billed Dowitchers, White Pelicans, Wilson's Phalaropes, a White-faced

Ibis, Caspian Terns, Western Grebes, a couple of Coots. You get the idea. Plus a River Otter! Nice stop.

We checked into the Quality Inn in Klamath Falls and walked about nine blocks to Antonio's Italian Kitchen for dinner. We went back to the motel and sent some more postcards via Amazingmail.com. Our species total for Oregon stood at 64 according to the computer. We planned to drive down to a couple of refuges just inside California the next morning and see what we could see.

We got breakfast at the Quality Inn around six – we were the only ones up at that hour. We filled up our gas tank and headed down Rte. 97 to California. Spent the next five or six hours birding Lower Klamath NWR, Tule Lake NWR, and Lava Beds National Monument. We got a total of forty-nine species for the morning, including a bunch that were new for this trip. In fact, our trip total was up to 87 species. Not bad for a couple of old poops. Oh yeah, we also saw several Mule Deer, a Coyote, [both at Lower Klamath] and a couple of Cottontails. Oh, and numerous California Ground Squirrels. [both at Tule Lake NWR] We went back to the motel after lunch at Schlotzky's. Sue did a bunch of laundry. I took a nap.

We started the day with breakfast at the Quality Inn in Klamath Falls. As we were returning to our room to get ready to go, a Great Horned Owl flew up onto an electrical wire right in front of us. How cool was that?

We spent most of the day driving clear across Oregon from south to north. We drove the Cascade Lakes Highway and made stops at Lava Lake, Hosmer Lake, Elk Lake and Sparks Lake. We got quite a few new birds – the trip total was up to 92, the Oregon list had hit 74. Most surprising bird of the day would have been the Wilson's Snipe at Elk Lake.

We chatted briefly with a couple who were volunteering there with the Passport in Time program.

192

The Cascade Lakes Highway ran through huge fields of poeoe or whatever they call big chunks of broken lava.

We stopped for lunch at the Deschutes Brewery and Pub in Bend. Good food, and they had the Eagles game on one of the TVs. Unfortunately, the Eagles looked awful and lost the game on a late field goal by Green Bay. Poop. We drove up to The Dalles, which was on the Columbia River. We were staying at another Comfort Inn. Had a light supper at the Shilo Inn across the road. We were pretty tired.

We had breakfast at the motel and drove across the bridge into Washington. We stopped at Catherine's Creek for a bit of birding. It wasn't dripping with birds, but we got a Black-throated Gray Warbler, which was a lifer for both of us. Yay. We stopped at several other spots recommended on the Washington Birding Trail brochure. We picked up a few birds at each place, including some Band-tailed Pigeons at Beacon Rock State Park.

We tried stopping at Ridgefield NWR near Vancouver, but it was really trashy, so we simply left. We ended up with 28 birds for the day. Lunch was fried chicken from a convenience store along Rte. 4 – we had a picnic at the Julia Butler Hansen National Wildlife Refuge for Columbia White-tailed Deer (I may be close on that name.) We had dinner at the Azteca Restaurant across the road. Sue burned her hand on the plate and splashed margarita all over. We were a little drunk. So what?

In the morning we "did" Mt. St. Helens National Volcanic Monument. Started at the visitor's center, where a nice gentleman who was vacuuming the lobby pointed out the bird trail. The trees were full of Evening Grosbeaks, which I believed was a life bird for both of us. The trail also held some other nice surprises including a bunch of Bushtits and a couple of Red-breasted Sapsuckers. Lifer number two for the day.

Our next stop was at Coldwater Lake, which was formed as a result of the big eruption of 1980. The lake was beautiful and we got a Common Loon and a trio of Killdeer along with more usual suspects. Continuing on to the Johnston Ridge Observatory, we had spectacular views of the volcano. The movie at the visitor's center was well worth seeing. The swarms of insects around the trail were not. We managed to find some perfect kitsch at one of the gift shops – a small glass vial of Mt. St. Helens ash.

We next hit the road for Mt. Rainier, and arrived there around three in the afternoon. We were staying at the inn in the park at Longmire. While sitting on the back porch that afternoon we saw a flock of Vaux's Swifts fly over. Lifer number three for the day.

We had a very nice dinner at the restaurant downstairs. Then we walked the Trail of the Shadows and the Gods of Birding showed us a Varied Thrush. He was just standing in the trail in front of us! That would be lifer number four for the day, but who was counting? I need to say a bit more about this bird and our encounter. Some of you may recall many pages ago when we saw our first Verdin and I didn't know what it was. Sue said, "Look in your guide book under Verdin." Ouch. I got to return the favor today when she didn't recognize the Varied Thrush. In fact I used her exact phrasing. To her credit, she did not hit me.

Next morning we drove up to Paradise. Stopped along to way to take numerous pictures of waterfalls and such. Then headed down to Ohanapecosh and the Grove of the Patriarchs. We stopped at the visitor's center at Ohanapecosh and walked the nature trail there. There was not a lot of avian activity in the forest, but we had one of our occasional birding thrills when we spotted an American Dipper hopping on the rocks in the river. He obliged with a brief display of walking on the river bottom while foraging. Wow.

We went from there to the Grove of the Patriarchs – a stand of thousand-year-old trees that was well worth the hike. They were repairing the footbridge to the grove, so there was an improvised log bridge that ended near a nasty-looking bee's nest. Someone had put up a hand-lettered sign that read "Caution: Bees." The old trees were pretty impressive. Even the dead ones. Sue took a picture of one dead log that had young trees growing out of the side of it.

We returned to the inn by about two and had a bite to eat. Actually, we both ordered sandwiches and ate only half, so we saved the rest for later if we felt like it. We walked the Trail of the Shadows again and got good looks at two Varied Thrushes this time. Sue tried to take a picture, but the birds were fast and the camera was slow. Alas. We found a present for our grandson, Colin, in the General Store. Had tea and scones on the porch. Thinned out our pictures and updated the bird list – we now had our fifty birds for Washington. The Dipper was number fifty. How cool was that?

We walked a little bit on the Trail of the Shadows again the next morning. Saw another Varied Thrush, but not much else. Most of the rest of the day was spent driving to Port Angeles.

We stopped and walked part of the trail at Dungeness NWR, about fifteen miles east of there. The Juan de Fuca Strait was completely fogged in, but we managed to locate a Winter Wren in the forest. Walked around Port Angeles a little. We drove up to the visitor center for Olympic National Park. Found a patch for our collection and a bucket hat for Syd. Had a late lunch/early dinner at Michael's Divine Dining. I had the beet and walnut soup (sounded weird, tasted good) and a fried oyster po'boy. Sue had three-cheese ravioli. Good food and reasonable. We have been catching up on email after having been offline for two days. I had a

195

total of 101 messages to wade through. Mostly bird alerts and spam.

We got an early start the next morning despite the unpromising look of the weather. It was overcast and cool when we started out, with fog out on the bay and up in the mountains. However, we decided to drive up to Hurricane Ridge in Olympic National Park and see what we could see. About two thousand feet up the mountain we emerged ABOVE the fog. It was clear and sunny up there! On the way up we saw two female Blue Grouse. Lifer! There were also a lot of small deer on the way up, but we aren't sure what species. Possibly Roosevelt.

In any case, we walked one of the loop trails on the ridge and headed back down. We stopped to take a few pictures on the way and picked up a couple more birds. We think we saw a Red Crossbill, but we couldn't really be sure, so it didn't count.

The next hour and a half or so was spent driving around the peninsula to Rialto Beach. The bay was alive with birds. We got two lifers – Common Murre and Marbled Murrelets. Plus there were Brown Pelicans, Pelagic and Double-crested Cormorants. Wait! We got Northwestern Crows, too. That would be three lifers. We also saw a couple of Harbor Seals and three or four dolphins just off the beach. We now had 62 birds for Washington and 115 or so for the trip.

Sue called Northwest Airlines that afternoon to see whether we could fly home a day earlier than originally planned. We could do that for a thousand bucks. Not likely!

We had a late breakfast for us. Around 6:30. First stop for the day was the Hoh Rainforest in Olympic National Park. It wasn't exactly raining, but it was overcast and misty. The forest itself was pretty impressive. Two hundred-foot tall trees. Zillions of different mosses and epiphytes growing on everything.

196

There was a dearth of avifauna in evidence that morning, but the hike was still worth it. At one point we heard a bull elk bugling not too far from us. We also saw a few Black-tailed Deer on the way in.

The rest of the day was mostly spent making our way to Westport, where we were spending two nights at the Alaskan Motel. We stopped to check out Ruby Beach and added Black Scoters to our Washington and trip lists. Made our way to Gray's Harbor NWR which had a colorful café at the entrance. Well, the refuge bordered an airfield, and the café was for that, I suppose. The place was called Lana's Hangar Café, and the décor was American Diner throughout with an aviation theme. Pictures of Betty Boop outside and in. Model airplanes hanging from the ceiling. An old car grille over the counter. Newspaper stories about the logging industry under the glass tabletops. American Eclectic.

Most of the birds we saw there were on a sewage lagoon. We added a bunch of waterfowl to our lists. In Westport we checked into the Alaskan Motel and the owner was most helpful with information about local restaurants and where to catch our boat in the morning.

We wandered around town a bit. Found out the Westwind Restaurant was open for breakfast at 4:30. Most others were at six or seven or even nine on Sunday. Looked like we'd be heading for the Westwind in the morning. We located the pier from which our trip would leave the next day, so we were ready to see some pelagic birds!

Dinner that evening was at the Castaways Restaurant in town. The waitress was brusque but pleasant. The food was good. Sue had a barbecued beef brisket sandwich. I had a basket of clam strips and fries.

The next day was our planned and pre-paid pelagic trip out of Westport. And I do mean paid. In

197

order to take the trip at all, we had to join the Washington Ornithological Society. I think that had something to do with insurance. Then there was the cost of the trip itself. If we were the sort of birders who evaluate our travels on the basis of cost per bird, this would have been an expensive outing! It's only money.

We got up around a quarter to five and got to breakfast at the Westwind by 5:15 or so. We had large breakfasts in case they didn't feed us on the boat. They didn't, but we had fruit and munchies with us, so we were fine. There were about twenty-five birders and three or so spotters/guides. The sea was calm when we started at 6:30 and stayed reasonably smooth all day. It rained lightly toward the end of the trip, but it wasn't too bad. The birding was incredible. We had a total of 29 species that included eight life birds! They would be: Sabine's Gull, Pink-footed Shearwater, Short-tailed Shearwater, Cassin's Auklet, Rhinoceros Auklet, Tufted Puffin, Black-footed Albatross and Fork-tailed Storm-petrel. Plus we saw a large pod of Rossi's Dolphins (formerly known as Gray Grampus) one Elephant Seal, a Steller's Sea Lion, a couple of Harbor Seals and a few Harbor Dolphins, a Northern Fur Seal, and three or four Ocean Sunfish. A good day! Cost per bird: Who cares?

Talking to some of the Washington birders, we learned that they enjoyed making up names for common birds that sounded vaguely legitimate. The House Sparrow seemed to be a favorite. Some of the suggested names included: Dumpster Finch, Urban Grosbeak, and Black-throated Brown. I liked the way these guys thought! We stopped and had a light supper at Barbara's By the Sea.

We had breakfast in Westport at King's Waffle House. Had a nice chat with our waitress. There was only one other customer, and he got take-out. The weather was giving us a taste of Northwest clouds and rain. Traffic was awful on I-5, but we had time to kill.

We stopped at the airport and asked about getting an earlier flight home. No soap. No flight, either. So we marked time until the following evening when our original flight was to leave at around 10 PM. Lunch at Metzel's across the street from the motel.

After breakfast at the Comfort Inn we loaded the car and headed in to Seattle. Found a free parking garage near Kent Station. Bought train tickets to take us downtown. Then realized that the trains only ran during rush hour, which it wasn't. Fourteen bucks down the toilet. We caught a bus instead and it took about forty-five minutes to get there. We took the monorail (originally built for the 1962 World's Fair) – a ride of roughly two minutes – and then visited the Space Needle. I went up to the observation deck and the views of Puget Sound were spectacular. We found a patch for our collection and a Space Needle snow storm/ring toss thingy for our Seattle kitsch. Took the monorail back into town and walked over to the Pike Place Market.

Had a nice lunch at the Soundview Café – I had a shrimp cocktail and a cup of clam chowder. Sue had chicken quesadillas. I ate one just to help her out. We checked out a Northwest Indian Art gallery and Sue bought a couple of prints. We wandered on to Pioneer Square and from thence to the train station. We thought maybe we could use half of our round-trip tickets. Alas, the first train to Kent Station did not leave until 4:20. It was only 2, so we caught another 150 bus and returned to the car.

# Chapter 25
## Return to Florida and Georgia
### February 24 – March 2, 2008

At the end of February, 2008, Sue's sister, Paula passed away after a long fight with cancer. We had tickets to attend several Phillies spring training games in Clearwater, Florida, so we decided to drive to Chicago for the funeral and then drive from there down to Florida (rather than going back home in between.)

The day after the funeral we covered a total about 650 miles and found ourselves that evening in Chattanooga, TN. We saw a lot of Red-tailed Hawks along the way and not much else. The weather was bitterly cold in Indiana – the temperature dipped to 7° F. at one point. It climbed to about 50° by the time we got to southern Tennessee.

We had breakfast at our hotel in Chattanooga and then stopped at a self-serve car wash to get the worst of the salt and dirt off, because Sue's motto is "A Clean Car is a Happy Car." We were on the interstate by a few minutes after eight and spent the day driving across Georgia. Along the way we picked up a Canada Goose for our 51st bird in Georgia.

We made it to the Tampa Bay area around five. Stopped at the El Cheapo Inn in Largo where we had reservations. It was filthy, so we checked out nearly as soon as we checked in and spent the next hour driving around the area looking for an alternate place to stay. Ended up at the Best Western Yacht Harbor in Dunedin. It was *clean* and right on the Gulf of Mexico. Not cheap. We had our room until Friday morning, but the place was fully booked for the weekend. We thought we would check out the Holiday Inn Express up the road and stay there on Friday night. Then we could get a head start on our drive home after the game on Saturday. Oh, we saw some nice birds whatever day that was, including several Ospreys, one Oystercatcher, a few Brown Pelicans and a

Loggerhead Shrike. We were tired for some reason. How many miles did we drive?

Sue took her car to a Saturn dealer the next morning and got an oil change. I stayed at the Best Western and did some birding around the neighborhood. Got some good birds, too – Little Blue Heron, White Ibis, Common Loon, Belted Kingfisher, Ospreys, Ruddy Turnstones, Willets, you get the picture. When Sue returned we drove up to Honeymoon Island and walked the Osprey Trail. We got 21 species even though it was the middle of the day. Lots of nesting Ospreys, a Palm Warbler, some Yellow-rumps, a Common Ground-dove, Common Tern, and we heard a number of Eastern Towhees.

From there we went up to Tarpon Springs where we had lunch at a Greek restaurant cleverly named "Mr. Greek." I had pickled octopus for an appetizer. We had a good meal for a reasonable price. Then we went back to our room. Sue did laundry and I napped and dumped pictures onto the computer. We walked over to downtown Dunedin that evening and managed to shop without buying a thing.

The temperature dropped about thirty degrees by morning and the wind was been between 20 and 30 miles per hour. We still went for a bird walk in the neighborhood and got about twenty species. Then we drove down to the ballpark early and watched batting practice.

We got really cold at the game, so we left after five innings. The Phillies were leading the Reds 3-0 when we left. We went up to the Dunedin Causeway afterwards to check out the shorebirds. There were dozens of Black Skimmers along with some other nice birds. A couple of Oystercatchers. Two or three Marbled Godwits. That sort of thing.

We had both eaten cheesesteaks at the baseball game and so we just had a light supper at the hotel.

The piano player was a woman who seemed to talk more than she played, which was OK because her playing was mediocre on her good numbers. The bass player was much better.

We got up the next morning around seven. After breakfast we drove up to Tarpon Springs and tried to find the Anklote River Park or Preserve or whatever it was called. We were using a useless Tarpon Springs brochure. We even stopped and asked directions. No luck. Finally decided to try the Brooker Creek Preserve instead. Got some nice birds there – Blue-headed Vireo and Yellow-bellied Sapsucker come to mind.

Then we headed for the ballpark. It was warmer only because of lower wind velocities. Our seats were in the shade, and we eventually moved to empty seats in the sun. Ryan Howard hit a monster home run with two on, but the Phillies were trailing the Pirates 8-5 when we left after the seventh inning. By that time there were no players on the field that we had ever heard of.

We had a little treat that evening when a small group of Roseate Spoonbills showed up out behind our room. Our species list for the trip was up to 64 at that point.

Our quest the next day was to get as many birds as possible since we had no species for February 29 ever. A couple of Wood Storks flew by while we were eating breakfast. A good omen from the Gods of Birding.

Then we drove up to Brooker Creek Preserve. We ran into a local birder there and we had a nice visit. Also got some good birds there again – Bald Eagle, Northern Parula, Blue-gray Gnatcatchers, Ruby-crowned Kinglet.

Next we drove all the way up to Crystal River and checked out one of the nature preserves. It was around noon, so we didn't get many birds, but a few good new ones for the day list – Eastern Bluebirds, Hermit Thrush, Towhees.

Then we headed south again and stopped at King's Bay. This time we weren't looking for birds, we were looking for Manatees. It turned out there were at least a dozen of them feeding right near an observation pier at the visitor's center. Wowowowow. What a thrill! We finished up our trail food and got a patch and a pin at the shop there. I went back out to the pier and watched them for a few more minutes. What wonderful and bizarre critters they are.

We headed back to Dunedin and stopped at the causeway to make sure we got over fifty birds for the day. We ended up with 58. Good day.

We went for a bird walk after breakfast. When we got the car packed, Sue suggested we skip the ballgame and get on the road toward home. I had no problem with that, so we gave our tickets to a couple in the breakfast room and started out around nine. Crossing Georgia, we spotted some American Coots for #52 for that state. Ten hours later we stopped in Lumberton, NC and checked into a Comfort Inn. The good news was they had a smoking room. The bad news was it wasn't too clean. Cleaner than the Cheapo Inn in Clearwater, but not spotless. Acceptable, however. It was only for one night! We decided to find some dinner locally and had more trouble than we needed after our day. The first place had a significant waiting line. The second place offered us a table next to a whiny folksinger with an amplified guitar. The table farther away had "already been requested" so we simply walked out. The third place turned out to be a big buffet, once again with a long line. No thanks. We don't do buffets any more. So we ended up having sandwiches at the local Quizno's. They were tasty, although not what we had had in mind for a nice dinner. We were too tired to care. We had driven over 560 miles, and I suspect we were less than half way home.

We hit the road in North Carolina a little after 6:30 next morning. Traffic wasn't outrageous and the weather was mild and sunny so we made good time. Pulled into our garage a few minutes after three. Glad to be home.

## Chapter 26
## Birding the Heartland
## Kansas, Oklahoma, Arkansas and Missouri
## Thursday, April 24 – Saturday, May 3, 2008

We were getting near the end of our quest. We had found our fifty species in 45 states. All that were left were Kansas, Oklahoma, Arkansas, Missouri and Alaska. We decided to save Alaska for last. It seemed fitting to end the quest with a bang. While surfing the web we found a birding festival scheduled for late April and early May in Kansas. They promised there would be a special excursion one morning to watch Greater Prairie Chickens displaying on their lek. That seemed like a wonderful excuse to go to Kansas and an easy way to get fifty species. Birding festivals are notoriously loaded with local birders, and even if we couldn't find fifty species on our own, the field trips should do the trick.

As long as we were travelling to the heart of America, Sue figured she might as well plan a sort of grand finale trip to finish up the lower forty-eight. Do the festival in Kansas, drop down and do Oklahoma, scoot over to Arkansas and return to Missouri to fly home from Kansas City. Out came the maps. Online she went. It didn't take long for the Master Trip Planner to come up with a detailed itinerary that looked likely to accomplish our goal.

We got up around our usual 6 a.m. and hit the road by a little after seven. Got to the airport a little after eight. Our plane left just before eleven. There were not many people around the Philly airport that morning. We got to Memphis about half an hour early (about 12:15 Central Time.) Since our connecting flight wasn't until just before three, we had a nice lunch at the Blue Note in the airport and then made our way to our gate. We still had plenty of time, so we took turns wandering and reading.

Got to Kansas City, MO around four-thirty that afternoon. Our baggage showed up quickly and we picked up our car at Advantage and hit the road. We got a few birds along the way (fifteen species, to be precise) including a couple of nice ones – Belted Kingfisher and American Kestrel spring to mind. There were numerous billboards along I-70 advertising the "Oz Museum" in Wamego. One urged us to call 1-866-458-TOTO. Seriously. I almost wished we had a cell phone. The operative word in that sentence was "almost" in case you missed it.

We spent the first of three nights at a Comfort Inn in Junction City, KS. It was not stunningly clean, but cleaner than some motels we have stayed in. Couldn't beat the price. We were using up our Choice Club points or whatever they were called, which meant the room was free.

Dinner was at the Washington Street Grille and Pub in town. I continued my sociological research in the Midwest by ordering single malt Scotch. Unlike the "single mulch" experience in Nebraska, they had six or seven choices! I ordered a Macallan's straight up. I got what looked like at least a double. No, I don't remember what I was charged for it. More than $3, I'm sure. There was a huge flock of Chimney Swifts in town. Our Kansas species total was up to 17. It was a start.

We took our time getting started the next morning, which means we didn't get to breakfast until around seven. Then we drove up to the other side of Junction City to check out the river walk hiking trail just outside the Fort Riley compound. Of course we missed our turn and ended up at the entrance to Fort Riley. A dear friend of ours had served at Fort Riley during the Korean War as a combat trumpeter. As he was quick to point out, "You never heard of the Chinese Communists invading Kansas, did you?" We had to make a u-turn. It was drizzling, so we went back to the hotel to get our rain jackets.

When we actually started hiking the trail, we found some good birds, including our first *Kansas* Indigo Bunting. After about a half mile or so we realized that we had forgotten to lock the car. Aargh. So we walked back and, um, locked the car. While we were there, I also got the GPS reading from the receiver I had left on the dash. It made me feel doubly stupid to have left an expensive electronic toy in the unlocked car. No harm, no foul. We ended up hiking about a mile and a half or so and finding about thirty species of birds. Our favorites for the walk were Black-and-white Warblers, a Great-crested Flycatcher, and a colony of Bank Swallows.

After covering most of that trail twice, we were tired, so we returned to the hotel for a bit of rest. Around noon we headed up to Wakefield, where the birding festival was headquartered. We got there too early to register, so we drove around the park along the Milford Reservoir and checked out the Kansas Landscape Arboretum. The arboretum looked like a work in progress, although it was established in 1972. Not that we spent much time there nor walked the trails, but it had an unfinished feel about it. They did have a trail called "The Bird Sanctuary Trail" but we didn't take the time to walk it. In spite of our laziness, we got our fiftieth Kansas bird around 12:45. Anything we saw after that was gravy.

Registration for the festival began around noon, but the first actual activity didn't start until four. What did we do to kill the time? We parked by the reservoir and napped until 3:30 or so. Did I mention that it was very windy all day? Steady wind of around twenty miles per hour with higher gusts. As a result, the festival leaders decided to simply take everyone to sheltered areas (well, out of the wind, anyway) to see what we could find. We got a bunch more birds and ended the afternoon with 81 birds on our Kansas list. 76 species just for the day.

Rising around 4:30 the next morning, we were on the road to Wakefield about five of five. Breakfast was at the Birding Festival headquarters in the Methodist Church. They had biscuits and gravy, scrambled eggs, coffee, tea, juice and pastries.

Our excursion to the Konza Prairie Biological Station left a few minutes after six – three vans with about thirty birders and guides. It took nearly an hour to get to the prairie where we were met by a couple of docents. The station was closed to the public except when accompanied by someone officially connected with the place. However, their website indicated that trails were open to the public from dawn to dusk and they even published online self-guided hikes. Whatever. We spent the morning – until 11 or so – driving around the Bison Loop. Along the way we saw lots of Bison (no kidding!) and a dozen or so White-tailed Deer. There were not many birds in evidence, although we saw lots of Upland Sandpipers, dozens of Eastern Meadowlarks, plus numerous sparrows of at least seven different species. Lunch was at the Hokansen Homestead where there was a walking trail and some outdoor seating for picnickers. The trees around the homestead were a welcome break from the tall grass prairie.

On the whole, the trip took much longer than it needed to. We did add six new species to our Kansas list which now stood at 87.

On the way back to Wakefield we stopped and got great looks at a baby Great-horned Owl. I saw his mama, too, although no one else mentioned seeing her. We had lunch with the group at the church and then went back to our hotel and rested most of the afternoon. Oh, we stopped at Wal-Mart and Sue got us gloves for the next morning. We would be sitting in a blind waiting for Greater Prairie Chickens to display and it was supposed to be pretty cold.

The banquet that evening was entertaining. The food was down home and plentiful. Before we ate they introduced every minor politician in two or three counties. In fact, the mayor of Clay Center and her husband sat at our table. Speaking of down home. The after-dinner speaker was a professor from Kansas State who shared pictures and stories from his 2005 sabbatical spent mostly in Utah. He had some terrific pictures and his style was self-deprecating and very funny. At one point he speculated on whether Magpies had some form of religion, since they seemed to gather around fallen comrades and mourn their passing. Sounded sort of forced to me. Silly, even.

Afterward they had all sorts of door prizes to give away. A bag of goodies from the Nature Conservancy. Copies of Aldo Leopold's *A Sand County Almanac.* The centerpieces from the tables. You get the idea. I felt a bit like I had been transported back to the 1950s again. This was not a bad thing. One of the local birders had a very broad accent. Our favorite example was his referring to Double-crested *Coomerants.*

We got up at three next morning and hit the road by about half past. Got to the Methodist church in Wakefield right at four and were the first "customers" for breakfast. The ladies had made a couple of different casseroles involving eggs and meat. They made for a good, hearty breakfast. The group left for the Prairie Chicken lek at around quarter to five. It turned out to be on the Fort Riley Military Reservation across Rte. 77 from Wakefield. We got to the blind by five-thirty. Roughly built of unfinished timber, it had a space of about four feet by maybe ten or twelve. Eight or nine of us – some with scopes and/or serious camera lenses – crammed in there and waited for the sun and the chickens to appear. The crowding was actually a good thing. The heat from our bodies took the edge off the chill in the air.

The birds showed up as soon as the sun cast the first suggestion of dawn across the lek. There were about ten males and a couple of females as far as I could tell. The males were competing to impress the females by inflating the orange air sacs on their throats, erecting the feathers on the back of their heads so they looked a bit like rabbit ears, drooping their wings and stamping and calling and hopping around. It was an impressive display, and they did it twice with a brief intermission between shows. Woooow.

We spent the rest of the morning birding around the reservation (Sue and I were ready to leave after the chicken display, frankly) and did see more interesting birds – a Bald Eagle on her nest for example. We made our way back to Wakefield by about 11:30 and Sue and I started driving to Oklahoma. We decided to take Rte. 77 down to I-35. It was the shortest route and the drive was much more pleasant than taking I-70 and I-whatever. We saw a couple of new Kansas birds along the way – Golden Eagle and Hooded Merganser come to mind. By the time we reached OK our Kansas list hit 97 species. Maybe we should have gone for 100...

Once in OK we drove over to Salt Plains NWR and birded along the nature trail there. We got a Red-headed Woodpecker right at the entrance. Then came White-faced Ibis, Little Blue Herons, American Avocets, and so much more!

It was getting late (5:30 or so) so we decided we'd better head for Enid, where we were staying with our first Evergreen Club hosts.

We called from Nash, OK, which isn't really much of a town, but did have one of those quaint public conveniences known as a pay telephone.[13] Along the way we saw the sign of the day: "Ballerina Mobile Home Country Club." Huh? When we got to Enid we stopped at a convenience store to ask directions. Actually, Sue stopped to ask directions. The folks in the store didn't know how to find their own butts, but a kindly older gentleman outside had a map of the town and showed Sue how to get to Seneca Ave. Of course,

---

[13] I didn't get a cell phone until 2010.

we had the address wrong on our itinerary. It showed up as 207, whereas it is actually 2007, so that little glitch necessitated another phone call. We finally got there around seven-thirty. Bill and Sheryl had a nice ranch-style home and we were housed in a separate wing with our own bed and bath room. We were tired for some reason.

We (read Sue) did a lot of driving the next day. Had a nice breakfast with Bill and Sheryl as well as a pleasant visit. Hit the road about 8:30 or so and drove over to Sequoyah NWR via Tulsa and Muskogee. Sign of the day was at a combination restaurant and gas station named "Tuck-a-Tummy." It was along the Cimarron Parkway near Tulsa. We also noted a billboard advertising "jesusdoesnotcare.com." Haven't checked that website yet. The wildlife refuge was very nice and we got some great birds, including two Bald Eagles, a Prothonotary Warbler, a couple of Northern Parulas, and a Scissor-tailed Flycatcher.

We walked the nature trail and then left so we could get to the Spiro Mounds State Park. It was closed. Crap. So we decided to drive up to Sallisaw to check out an advertised Indian souvenir store. Couldn't find it. Double crap. So we drove down to Poteau and checked in to the Best Western. Then we went "downtown" looking for a restaurant and maybe a store to buy an Oklahoma souvenir. Found an interesting "Choctaw medicine stick" but I decided since the "wolf skull" was made of plastic it might not be too authentic. Did buy a turtle shell rattle for ten bucks. Oh, all the "nice" restaurants in the area are closed on Monday. Nertz. So we got sandwiches at the local Subway and ate in our room.

We checked out of the Best Western in Poteau, OK after breakfast and headed down to Talihina where we filled the gas tank in our rental car. Went back up to the visitors' center for the Talimena Scenic Drive (sometimes called a Scenic Byway and formerly known as the Talimena Skyline Drive) and of course it was closed. Evidently we are spending a couple of days in the part of Oklahoma that doesn't open until Wednesday. The scenic drive was open, but not the visitor's center.

The good news is we got a Summer Tanager behind the visitor's center. We saw some other nice birds along the byway, including a singing male Scarlet Tanager and three Greater Roadrunners! I don't know why, but we weren't expecting Roadrunners this far east. By the time we crossed into Arkansas, we had 75 species for Oklahoma. We stopped on the Arkansas side and walked a little half-mile nature trail (the Earthquake Ridge nature trail) that produced a Red-eyed Vireo, and a Pine Warbler among others. Along the way to Hot Springs we passed the "Little Hope Baptist Church." No comment necessary.

In Hot Springs we walked around downtown a bit and found a shop with souvenir patches and an Arkansas Razorback nose for my kitsch collection. Then we looked for a place for lunch. The first two places we tried each had only one employee on duty and completely dysfunctional rest rooms. The third place had several waitresses and working toilets, so we ate there.

Then we checked out the Hot Springs National Park visitors' center. Watched the movie. Looked in the main bath room (there is a break there) and took some pictures. Drove up the mountain and hiked around a bit. Best bird was a Hooded Warbler. Went down to Lake Catherine State Park, since we had time to kill, and it turned out to be further away than we thought. Did get a Ruby-throated Hummingbird there, though. New for Arkansas!

Back into town where we had a nice dinner at The Brickhouse – outstanding steaks and a lively waiter who let us use his cell phone to call Don and Vera P, with whom we were spending the night. The P's live in

Hot Springs Village, a gated community. Don met us at the Remax office and led us to their place. Spent an hour and a half or so visiting. They were very nice and their home was lovely. We dumped our pictures from the day onto the laptop and headed for sleep.

We got up around 6:30 and Vera had breakfast ready by 7 as promised. It consisted of biscuits, boiled eggs with bacon bits, coffee, and chocolate muffins. Very nice. As are Don and Vera. I didn't mention it yesterday, but Vera paints on blue eyebrows. Other than that, she looks like a normal octogenarian. Just a guess. Don took us on a drive around part of the "village" so we could see the lake. We turned around at "Cloaca Lane." I wonder who chose that name?

Anyway, we were on our way to Holla Bend NWR by about 8:15. Holla Bend, by the way was near Dardanelle, home of the Dardanelle Sand Lizards. The birding there was wonderful, even though we arrived around 10. Our favorite species had to be the dozens of singing Dickcissels. Oh, and some Bobwhites and Blue Grosbeaks. Plus a Box Turtle. Sometime in the course of our tour of the auto route we hit our fiftieth Arkansas bird, so it was time to move on.

Spent the rest of the afternoon driving to Nevada, MO. Stopped near Joplin for dinner at an Applebee's. Checked our email and got directions to our Evergreen place for the following night. Oh, we ended up with 59 species in Arkansas. Currently had a twelve-species start on Missouri.

After breakfast at the Country Inn and Suites we decided to check out a couple of Wildlife Areas we had seen signs for off Rte. 71. We couldn't find the Gay Feather Wildlife Refuge and the Osage Prairie Wildlife Refuge was not too promising given the twenty to thirty mile-per-hour winds. So we headed up to the Schell-Osage Wildlife Management Area. It consisted of a series of lakes and ponds and wetlands and forest fragments. Highlights included a male Rose-breasted Grosbeak, a number of Spotted Sandpipers, a Pectoral Sandpiper, and a handful of Snow Geese who must not have decided to migrate yet. We saw two black rat snakes crossing the road at different times. We had fifty birds by the time we left there, so we headed up to Kansas City to check out a couple of promising places.

Eventually. Sort of. We kind of got lost on Route M. At least we didn't have a clear idea where we were, just the general impression that we were mostly headed west. This was good, because after a while we hit Rte. 71 and headed north. Had lunch at Arby's in Harrisonville.

Then we made our way to the James A. Reed Memorial Wildlife Area near Kansas City. There were lots of birds around and we picked up several more species – Harris' and Clay-colored Sparrow f'rinstance. Then we drove up to Blue Springs Lake where we found a small Audubon Center where we sat and watched their feeders while talking to a couple of ladies who evidently work there, presumably as volunteers. We got 21 species, including several new ones for our Missouri list. All while sitting on our bums.

From there we looked for another birding hotspot, but the directions were vague and we were tired so we headed for a local mall. Sue had her hair cut while I spent money at a local Border's Express. Dinner was at a generic restaurant named O'Charley's that could have been a Bennigan's or a Ruby Tuesday, or fill in your favorite. The food was good, though.

We were staying that night at Bob and Charlotte W's house, our third Evergreen stay. Bob was ill, so he was hiding in the basement. Charlotte was very nice and we traded world travel stories for an hour or so. I caught up our bird list and we had 68 species for Missouri. That meant we had successfully found at least 50 species in 49 out of 50 states. Next year – ALASKA!

The area was hit by severe thunderstorms overnight. In fact at least one tornado seemed to have touched down just north of where we stayed. Charlotte fixed a good breakfast for us – scrambled eggs and bacon. Bob made an appearance after we ate and said he was feeling a lot better. We chatted for a while and then started out to visit Independence.

We started at the visitor's center and then went over to have a tour of the Truman house where Harry and Bess lived before and after his presidency. The house itself reminded both of us of our grandparents' places right down to the smell. The most poignant moment for us was seeing Harry's hat and coat on the rack where he left them after his last walk around town. Then we went to his presidential library and museum. Lots of interesting exhibits as well as Harry and Bess's graves in the courtyard.

We had a bite to eat at a German restaurant near the visitors' center and then headed downtown to see the World War One memorial and museum. Charlotte had recommended it, and she was right. The building was beautiful and the exhibits incredible. We spent a couple of hours there and headed up to our hotel. Because of last night's storms, the internet connection did not seem to be working. Since we were flying home the next day, it wasn't critical. Of course, I DID want to email the credit union to tell them I lost my debit card the previous day. Didn't think anyone could use it without the PIN anyway, and I was too tired to care.

# Chapter 27
## Alaska at Last
### Thursday, May 14 – Friday, May 22, 2009

Our flight left Philadelphia over an hour late and we missed our connection, so we were stuck in Salt Lake City for one night. We were re-booked for a flight at 8:10 the next morning that would stop in Seattle on the way to Anchorage. We were not happy with Delta.

We got up around 5 AM Utah Time Friday and got the shuttle to the airport. Our flight to Seattle was on time. The plane was very cramped and our backpacks wouldn't fit in the overhead compartment. They didn't really fit under the seats, either, so we rode sort of scrunched up. In Seattle we had some time between flights to wander the airport and get a bite to eat. The flight to Anchorage left more or less on schedule, and we got there around 2:30 in the afternoon. The Ramada Inn shuttle was not running that afternoon (?!) so we were instructed to take a cab and they would pay the driver. That worked for us.

In any case, we were finally in Alaska. Interestingly it was the fiftieth anniversary of Alaskan statehood. Seemed sort of symmetrical that we were there to get fifty birds in our fiftieth state. We had some spectacular views of mountains and glaciers on the flight from Seattle. Once we took showers, we walked down to the bay to see what birds were about.

Anchorage still had a frontier feel to it. There was something raw and unfinished about the place. Some of the streets petered out into dirt tracks at the end. There was a lot of construction going on. Some new buildings, some seedy and old.

On our walk we got our first life birds in Alaska – Mew Gulls. We also found a shop run by native Alaskans called *Two Spirits Gallery and Art Center*. I bought a soapstone sculpture of a raven dancer and a smaller one of a sea otter. The raven dancer cost a bit more than I usually spend on souvenirs, but two things came into play. The first was my intention from the start to find a nice soapstone sculpture on this trip. The second was the fact that the day before I had discovered that my government "stimulus" check had been deposited in my bank account. So I did my part to help the country dig out of the recession. Who says that liberals are unpatriotic?

The group meeting that night was pleasant and the group seemed very congenial. There were eleven hostile elders plus two leaders – Kris C and Nan E. A very nice size for a birding group! The next day the weather pretty much stank. Cold. Rainy. Windy. We spent the morning birding our way from Anchorage to Moose Pass. Had a couple of very productive stops in spite of the weather. At Potter Marsh we got our first Arctic Tern for the trip along with Violet-green Swallows and a Canvasback. Gerdwood produced fourteen species including a Red-necked Phalarope, Gadwall, and Barrow's Goldeneye. We saw a Moose near the airport in Anchorage and a Muskrat at Potter Marsh.

After lunch at the Trail Lake Lodge in Moose Pass we drove to Seward and had a behind-the-scenes tour of the Alaska Sea Life Center. It was very impressive. The money for the facility came from the Exxon Valdez settlement. They took care of injured birds and mammals (mostly marine) as well as caring for a collection of critters on display to the public. We got to see a couple of Puffins and Auklets up close and personal.

Dinner at the lodge was followed by birding at Tern Lake. Best bird was a "heard only" Northern Saw-whet Owl. Seeing Common Loons in breeding plumage was also a treat. Oh, and a Varied Thrush singing from the top of a tree. A Bald Eagle near an active nest. Oh, and several Mountain Goats and a... I was too tired to write in more detail that night. It was nearly 10:30. It didn't get dark until around 2 and then it got light again around 4.

Beautiful weather the following day. Sunny and mild. We birded around Seward with Tasha from Alaska Sea Life Center all morning. Saw some good birds at a wetland near the airport – Arctic Terns, Greater White-fronted Geese, that sort of thing. The Canada Geese there seemed to be mostly the so-called Dusky subspecies – *Branta canadensis occidentalis*. At the dry dock on Nash St. we got several good birds: Pigeon Guillemot and Orange-crowned Warbler, Pectoral Sandpiper, Short-billed Dowitchers, lots of Bald Eagles.

After a light lunch of sandwiches and cookies at the Alaska Sea Life Center, the group drove out to Exit Glacier with the local Audubon lady, Carol. As we hiked around in Kenai Fjords National Park near the glacier and spotted a Ptarmigan 'way up one of the mountains. It was a tiny white speck. Neither Kris nor Nan cared to speculate on which species it might be. At that point, I knew our total species count for Alaska was close to fifty. I was hoping that the unidentified Ptarmigan was not going to turn out to be number fifty. Of course, since it was unidentified, it couldn't count as number fifty in any case. It turned out that a Spotted Sandpiper seen on our way in to the glacier was number fifty. So we had already (and unwittingly) achieved our goal. It had taken us thirteen years to get to that bird. To paraphrase T.S. Eliot, the quest ended not with a bang, but with a whimper. Well, more like a whisper. As birds are wont to do, the Spotty was simply feeding along the river amongst the stones at the edge of the Resurrection River. He wasn't wearing a special outfit to commemorate the occasion. He was unaware that we were even watching him.

Besides the significant bird, we got glimpses of two Black Bears, a Red-backed Vole, and unsurprisingly, another Moose today.

Dinner at Trail Lake Lodge was followed by a presentation by volunteers Dave and Beth from the Bird Treatment and Learning Center – Bird TLC for short. Beth showed us her Golden Eagle named Denali and talked about why he couldn't be released and how she takes care of him. At nine pounds, he is a big eagle! Dave was responsible for a Snowy Owl named Ghost. His description of caring for and training the bird to serve as an education specimen was interesting, if something of a grammatical adventure.

Our companions were all quite friendly and pleasant. There was Bill L, a biologist from Kansas who taught at Butler Community College in El Dorado. Chuck and Sally M from Shreveport, LA. Bill and Becky F who hailed from Bloomsburg, PA! A short blonde woman named Ria M who lived in Santa Barbara. I suspected "Ria" was short for Logorrhea, Ed and Sharon N who lived in Dallas, Sue B from San Diego who took a birding class at a local college and made up in enthusiasm what she lacked in knowledge.

The weather was stunning again the next morning. We took the Kenai Fjords National Park boat trip. There were several wonderful marine mammal encounters – first was a pod of Orcas swimming in company with Dall's Porpoises. Second was a group of three Orcas having sex – evidently it takes two females and a male. One female supports the other while she is copulating with the male. Last was a very close encounter with a female Humpback Whale and her calf. We got wonderful looks at both, including getting to see the head of the mother as she fed on the surface. We also saw a lot of good birds – Horned and Tufted Puffins in breeding plumage. Double-crested, Pelagic and Red-faced Cormorants. Common Murres. Black-legged Kittiwakes. We also spent some time at the Holgate Glacier where we got to see a couple of chunks calve off.

After we got back from the boat ride, Kris asked if we were up for one more bird before dinner. He took us to see a Dipper nest with two Dippers in the immediate vicinity! Plus, Bill  L spotted a Brown Creeper nearby. A few of us went for a bird walk after dinner and managed to find three Long-billed Dowitchers in perfect position to see the field marks that distinguish them from Short-billed. That doesn't happen very often!  Along the way I got a Savannah Sparrow. The group started up the mountain across the road from the lodge and got great looks at a pair of Varied Thrushes before I pooped out. Our Alaska list was up to 68 species. PDG. That's Pretty Damned Goods for those of you who just tuned in.

We spent the next day birding our way from Moose Bay to Homer, Alaska. We stopped at a number of places along the way and got a lot of good birds. In addition we saw 3 or 4 Moose, a couple of Red Squirrels, one Coyote, and three Caribou!

During a stop at Kenai Lake we saw a Dark-eyed Junco singing from the top of a spruce tree. Even though we see hundreds of Juncos every year in our back yard, we rarely hear them sing, and never see them exhibiting breeding behavior. We also got nice looks at a Pine Siskin and a Yellow-rumped Warbler besides the expected waterfowl on the lake.

Our group got fairly rowdy during the long rides between stops today. We were talking about getting songs stuck in our heads and Sue and I offered a rendition of our all-time worst – the Oscar Mayer bologna jingle. That triggered a series of sillier and sillier renditions of mostly advertising jingles by various members of the crew. It helped to pass the time.

We were staying at the Best Western Bidarka on the edge of Homer for the next few days. After dinner that evening, Kris and Nan took most of us on a sort of orientation drive around Homer. We drove the length of the longest man-made spit in the world. Stopped on the way back and got ice cream at a little shop called "Spit Licks." They weren't really open for the season yet, but were certainly willing to sell us cones. I tried the Kona Coffee flavor. Very good.

We spent the next morning birding around the Homer area with a local birder (and professional carpenter) named Dale. We got eight more birds for our Alaska list, and the most impressive had to be a pair of Parasitic Jaegers on their nest! As seemed to be usual in Alaska, we also saw two or three Moose.

In the afternoon we went to a presentation at the Alaska Islands and Oceans Center. They showed us a movie about the research being done in the Alaska Maritime NWR as well as a slide presentation.

After dinner about six of us went out to look for Saw-whet Owls on the trail by the Islands and Oceans Center. We saw Orange-crowned Warblers, Sandhill Cranes, Mallards, a Hermit Thrush, and a distinct dearth, a lack, and a paucity of Saw-whets. Bill L claims he saw about four last night. Harumph.

We birded around Kachemak Bay in the morning on a boat run by Karl Stolzfuss. Yes, he was a native Pennsylvania Dutchman. We saw lots of good birds and probably more than a hundred Sea Otters. We circumnavigated Gull Island, which contained thousands of Black-legged Kittiwakes, more thousands of Common Murres, plus good numbers of Red-faced and Pelagic Cormorants. That afternoon we checked out several local "hot spots" which turned out to be not so hot. Of course it WAS afternoon. We did add Gray Jays to our state list, which was up to 96 species. We also saw a couple of Moose and a Porcupine.

We took a second boat trip on Kachemak Bay with Karl Stolzfuss our last morning in Alaska. Got great looks at a Yellow-billed Loon. Also found a couple of Aleutian Terns resting on a piece of driftwood out in the bay. Both were lifers, of course. Also pushed our Alaska state list over the 100 species mark. Ended the day with 103. Along the way we saw lots of Sea Otters, several Harbor Seals, three or four Moose, including a cow about to have her calf. Also heard Wood Frogs at our last birding stop. It was easy to identify them, since they were the only amphibian that lived that far north in North America.

At supper that evening Sue B had bought champagne to celebrate the end of the trip plus a birthday cake for Sue M. A good time was had by all.

# Epilogue

So what did we do after Alaska? Life had lost a focus, a goal, a common project we loved working on together. Of course we continued birding. We still visited our favorite local birding spots again and again. Bombay Hook. Cape May. Tinicum. Local nature reserves. We also traveled to Europe (Greece, Scotland, England, Estonia, Netherlands, Ireland, Spain, Canary Islands, France) and we have birded in New Brunswick. Maybe fifty birds in each Canadian Province could be interesting. We still have only thirty-five species in Washington, DC. Plus, after it was all over we discovered that we had seen Rock Pigeons in 49 states. The missing one was a surprise – Louisiana! Surely we must have seen pigeons in New Orleans? If we did, I forgot to write them down. So those Louisiana pigeons don't exist. If there were any.

What about getting 100 birds in each state? We already have 100 in Alaska, Arizona, California, Delaware, Maryland, Montana, New Jersey, New Mexico, New York, North Carolina, North Dakota, Pennsylvania, Texas, Virginia and Wyoming. We have ninety-nine in Florida. Ninety-seven in Kansas. Ninety-two in Utah. Ninety-six each in Washington and Wisconsin. Somehow, now that we have visited all fifty states, returning to some to get more has less appeal. Too much "been there, done that" implied.

Some friends have suggested 100 birds in 100 countries. Or fifty birds in fifty countries. Maybe if we hit the lottery...

Our current quest is to record 100 species for every day of the year. No, not 100 birds on the same day, 100 birds recorded for each *date* no matter how many years it took to get them. We have (at this writing) completed 263 dates, including Leap Day. We are now planning our birding trips to coincide with days with fewer than 100...

223

# Appendix

Some of the places where we birded in the approximate order in which we finished each state:

1. **Pennsylvania**
   John Heinz NWR

   Hawk Mountain

   Stroud Preserve (Natural    Lands property near West Chester)

   Cheslen Preserve (Natural Lands property near our home)

   Hibernia County Park

   Marsh Creek State Park

2. **Delaware**
   Bombay Hook NWR

   Prime Hook NWR

   Little Creek Wildlife Area

   Indian River Inlet State Park

3. **New Jersey**
   Forsythe NWR

   Cape May (numerous sites)

   Barnegat ighthouse (Long Beach Island)

4. **New York**
   Montezuma NWR

   Labrador Unique Area

   Sapsucker Woods (Cornell University)

5. **Maryland**
   Conowingo Fisherman's Park

   Blackwater NWR

   Assateague Island National Seashore

   Eastern Neck NWR

6. **Virginia**
   Assateague/ Chincoteague Islands

224

Eastern Shore NWR

## 7. North Carolina
Pea Island NWR

Mackay Island

Coquina Beach

Cape Hatteras
National Seashore

## 8. New Mexico

Bosque del Apache
NWR

Rio Grande Nature
Center, Albuquerque

Water Canyon

Sandia Crest

Las Vegas NWR

## 9. South Carolina
Santee NWR

Carolina Sandhills
NWR

## 10. Georgia
Okefenokee Swamp

Savannah Area

## 11. Texas
Aransas NWR

Brazoria NWR

Choke Canyon State
Park

Attwater Prairie
Chicken NWR

## 12. Ohio
Ottawa NWR

Harrison Lake State
Park

## 13. Indiana
Indiana Dunes

## 14. Illinois
Chicago Botanic
Gardens

Evanston –
Northwestern
University Campus

## 15. Arizona
Boyce Thompson
Arboretum State
Park

Grand Canyon
National Park

Saguaro National
Park

Ramsey Canyon

San Pedro River
Conservation Area

16. **Rhode Island**
Trustom Pond NWR

Ninigret NWR

Sachuest NWR

17. **Florida**
Gulf Islands
National Seashore

Merrit Island NWR

Honeymoon Island
State Park

18. **Alabama**
Bon Secour NWR

Coastal Birding
Trail

19. **Mississippi**
Davis Bayou NWR

Grand Bay NWR

Mississippi Sandhill
Crane NWR

Ward Bayou NWR

20. **Louisiana**
Fontainbleau State

Park

Bayou Sauvage
NWR

Atchafalaya NWR

Big Branch Marsh
NWR

21. **Massachusetts**
Parker River NWR

Quabben Reservoir

22. **Vermont**
Missisquoi NWR

Mt. Ascutney State
Park

Wilgus State Park

23. **New Hampshire**
Great Bay NWR

Lake Umbagog
NWR

24. **Maine**
Acadia National
Park

Sunkhaze Meadows
NWR

25. **Connecticut**
Stewart B.
McKinney NWR

Rocky Neck State
Park

26. **Wyoming**
Grand Teton
National Park

Seedskadie NWR

Sinks Canyon State
Park

Yellowstone National
Park

27. **Idaho**
Bear Lake NWR

Gray's Lake NWR

28. **Utah**
Ouray NWR

Bear River Migratory
Bird Refuge

Golden Spike
National Monument

Farmington Bay
Waterfowl
Management Area

29. **Colorado**
Pawnee National
Grasslands

Rocky Mountain
National Park

Arapaho NWR

30. **Michigan**
Seney NWR

Shiawassee NWR

Grayling area

31. **Wisconsin**
Horicon NWR

Schlitz Audubon
Reserve

Wittlesy Creek NWR

Chiwaukee Nature
Preserve

32. **Minnesota**
Pipestone National
Monument

Sherburne NWR

Mille Lacs

33. **Nevada**
Ash Meadows NWR

Great Basin National
Park

Pahranagat NWR

34. **California**
Morro Bay

Joshua Tree
National Park

Lava Beds National
Monument

Lower Klamath NWR

Salton Sea

San Simeon State
Park

35. **West Virginia**
Cranesville Swamp

Blackwater Falls
State Park

Canaan Valley State
Park

Harper's Ferry

36. **Kentucky**
Clyde E. Buckley
Wildlife Sanctuary

Mammoth Cave
National Park

Land Between the
Lakes National
Recreation Area

37. **Tennessee**

Cross Creeks NWR

Tennessee NWR Big
Sandy Unit

Land Between the
Lakes National
Recreation Area

38. **Nebraska**
DeSoto NWR

Ft. Niobrara NWR

Rowe Sanctuary and
Audubon Center

Valentine NWR

39. **South Dakota**
Custer State Park

Lacreek NWR

40. **Iowa**
DeSoto NWR

Effigy Mounds
National Monument

Port Louisa NWR

Lake Red Rock

41. **Hawai'i**
Kapiolani Park
(Honolulu)

Paiko Lagoon
Wildlife Sanctuary
(Oahu)

Wahiawa Botanical
Gardens (Oahu)

Audubon Nature
Center at Waimea
Valley (Oahu)

Hanalei NWR
(Kaua'i)

Kilauea Lighthouse
Point NWR (Kaua'i)

Huleia NWR
(Kaua'i)

Hawai'i Volcanoes
National Park
(Hawai'i)

Kipuka Puaulu
Special Ecological
Area (Hawai'i)

Hakalau Forest
(Hawai'i)

## 42. **North Dakota**
Arrowwood NWR

Chase Lake NWR

Sully's Hill National
Game Preserve

Theodore Roosevelt
National Park

## 43. **Montana**
Glacier National
Park

Medicine Lake NWR

National Bison
Range

Ninepipes NWR

Owen Sowerwine
Natural Area

## 44. **Oregon**
Cape Meares

Crater Lake

Seal Rocks State
Park

Upper Klamath Lake

Yaquina Bay

## 45. **Washington**
Beacon Rock State
Park

Catherine's Creek
NWR

Julia Butler Hansen
NWR

Anchorage

Mt. Rainier National
Park

Homer

Kachemak Bay

Mt. St. Helen's
National Park

Kenai Fjords
National Park

Olympic National
Park

## 46. Kansas
Fort Riley Military
Reservation

Konza Prairie
Natural Area

## 47. Oklahoma
Salt Plains NWR

Sequoyah NWR

## 48. Arkansas
Holla Bend NWR

Hot Springs

## 49. Missouri
James A. Reed
Memorial Wildlife
Area

Schell-Osage
Wildlife Area

## 50. Alaska

Made in the USA
Middletown, DE
07 June 2020

96307344R00129